ULTIMATE GUIDE TO

Workers' Compensation

IN VIRGINIA

INJURED WORKERS'
LAW FIRM

Fourth Edition

ULTIMATE GUIDE TO

Workers' Compensation

IN VIRGINIA

MICHELE S. LEWANE, ESQ.

INJURED WORKERS'
LAW FIRM

ISBN: 978-1-59571-704-7

Designed and published by

Word Association Publishers
205 Fifth Avenue
Tarentum, Pennsylvania 15084

www.wordassociation.com
1.800.827.7903

TABLE OF CONTENTS

Why Did I Write This Book And Why Should You Read It?

I wrote this book because I have seen too many people victimized by insurance companies. I want to give injured workers knowledge that can help them in their battle with the insurance companies. Being informed is the most powerful weapon. Knowledge is power. You may not need an attorney to help you with your case but you need to be armed with this important information now before you make any important decisions about your case. I want injured workers to have good solid information BEFORE dealing with the insurance company, BEFORE hiring an attorney, and BEFORE settling their case.

The workers' compensation laws can be complicated and the Rules are ever changing. In fact, the laws have changed to such an extent, that I had to write this 4th Edition in just six (6) years since writing my original book. The insurance companies keep on top of the latest changes for their benefit and we need to be just as prepared.

This Is Not Legal Advice.

This book is not intended to be a substitute for legal advice from an experienced workers' compensation attorney—no book could fulfill such a function. If your injuries are serious and you have lost time from work, you should immediately seek counsel with a qualified workers' compensation attorney. However, if your injuries are minor and you haven't lost time from work, this book will help you protect your interests and receive your workers' compensation benefits without legal counsel. Please do not construe anything in this book to be legal advice specific to your case.

We Are Different.

My firm is different from a typical workers' compensation law firm. We do not take a large volume of cases and settle them cheaply without any intention of taking the cases to a hearing. Also, many times, clients come to us with cases for which they are clearly entitled to a recovery. However, because the injuries to the worker may be minor or they have not lost time from work, we may decide that it is their best interest and they will make more money not hiring an attorney and settling with the insurance company on their own. We tell our clients up front if hiring an attorney will get them more money. If we don't take your case, we give you guidance on how to settle your case on your own.

If your case does meet our requirements and we accept your case, you can be assured that your case will receive our personal attention. We will aggressively represent you, communicate with you frequently, and give you honest advice. We have been able to perfect the processes. This enables us to get your case done in the most expedient manner so you can get on with your life. Together, we will decide the best strategy to get you the highest recovery possible.

WARNING

Do not base any decision with respect to your case solely on any of the answers found in this book. Prior to making any decision regarding your case, you should speak with a competent attorney who is familiar with the Virginia Workers' Compensation system.

CHAPTER 1

Workers' Compensation Benefits

How It Began: The Triangle Shirtwaist Fire Of 1911

It has been over 100 years since the Triangle Shirtwaist Company factory fire in New York City on March 25, 1911. It was the deadliest industrial disaster in New York City until the September 11, 2001 World Trade Center terrorist attack. The fire killed 146 garment workers (mostly recent Jewish and Italian immigrant women aged 16–23). The factory made women's blouses on the 8th, 9th, and 10th floors of a building in Greenwich Village. The managers locked the doors to the stairwells and exits to prevent theft from the 500 workers and to allow managers to check the women's purses. The fire most likely started on the 8th floor where they cut the shirts, from an unextinguished cigarette butt in the scrap bin, which held 2 months worth of cuttings.

The 9th floor workers suffered the most deaths. The floor had two freight elevators, a fire escape, and stairways. The foreman who had the stairwell door keys escaped without opening the doors. Some survivors jammed themselves into the elevators until the elevators stopped working. The elevators stopped working when some women jumped into the empty shafts trying to slide down the cables, breaking the elevator cars.

While a crowd watched, 62 people jumped out of windows to their deaths to avoid being burned alive. A young man and woman were seen kissing at the window before both jumped to their death. The rest waited to be succumbed by smoke and fire.

The company owners were charged with manslaughter but were acquitted. In a civil suite in 1913, the plaintiffs won $75 per deceased victim. The shirtwaist company's insurance paid the owners $400 per lost victim (a $60,000 profit). Also in 1913, one of the owners was arrested once again for locking the doors in his factory during working hours and was fined $20. With public outrage and united unions, politicians started regulating businesses regarding worker safety, including creating the workers' compensation system.

What Is Workers' Compensation And Where Did It All Begin?

Workers' compensation in Virginia began in 1919 and is a no fault system. Workers' compensation is considered a compromise between employers and employees. It helps relieve hardship for an injured worker but does not give "full compensation." Prior to the enactment of the workers' compensation laws, to receive any type of benefits an employee had to show that the employer was negligent in failing to provide a safe work environment. Needless to say, this usually resulted in lengthy and expensive litigation that caused the employee and his family to suffer. Now, under workers' compensation, the employee receives benefits (a portion of his lost wages plus medical treatment) much faster and for less cost, without ever having to show the employer is negligent. However, as a result of this "compromise," an employee cannot recover compensation for pain and suffering. The employee gave up the possibility of getting a big financial windfall for immediate medical treatment and a portion of lost wages. On paper, this sounds like a fair compromise. However, what has happened through the years is that the insurance companies and large corporations have lobbied the Virginia General Assembly to carve away numerous exceptions that usually favor the employer over the employee. Not all accidents that happen at work are covered under workers' compensation. This means that now, when individuals get hurt at work, they not only have to deal with the their health issues and the financial burden of not working, but also, to get benefits, they have to fight the big businesses, big manufacturers, and big insurance companies- the same businesses which spend millions of dollars each year attacking and seeking to change the workers' compensation laws to benefit themselves and deprive injured individuals of their benefits. Insurance companies love to and are trained to "delay, delay, deny, delay..." This strategy and the workers' compensation rules favoring employers hurt injured workers even more.

Workers' compensation is governed by the Virginia Workers' Compensation Commission—not insurance companies. The Virginia Workers' Compensation Commission is a state agency. Everything must go through the Virginia Workers' Compensation Commission. Reporting your injury to your employer or filing a claim with the insurance company is not the same as filing a claim with the Virginia Workers' Compensation Commission. Check out their website at *www. vwc.state.va.us* for more information about the Commission.

How Do I Get Workers' Compensation Benefits?

In Virginia, to get workers' compensation benefits after you've been injured, you need to notify your employer immediately—even if you think it is a minor injury. Don't worry that you may not appear to be a "team player." Once your employer receives notice, he or she should file a first report of accident and submit it to the workers' compensation insurance carrier. At that point, the insurance adjuster will call you, ask questions about your injury, and record what you say. This is called a "recorded statement." I do not recommend that you agree to this, as it can be used against you, but you are almost never given a copy. When you start missing work, you should begin receiving two thirds of your wages weekly, and given a panel of three doctors. This may seem simple

BUT there are many traps. The biggest problem is that the injured worker has the burden of proof. This means that the insurance adjuster and the employer can do nothing and can say nothing. They have no obligation to explain anything to you, which may mislead you—and you have no recourse. It is up to the injured workers, even if he or she is unconscious in a hospital, to know what his or her rights and obligations are and to ask for benefits. Most insurance adjusters have a policy "if they don't ask, don't tell." This is the reason why it is best to talk to an attorney experienced in workers' compensation. You can find out what your rights are and be informed of any potential issues that could prevent you from getting your full benefits. You may not need to hire an attorney but you should get fully informed since you are held responsible for any mistakes you may make. Good workers' compensation attorneys will give you a free consultation to discuss your particular situation.

To What Type Of Benefits Am I Entitled?

If the injured worker meets his burden and proves that he does have a compensable work injury he may have the following six key benefits:

1. **Lost wages.** The legal term for complete lost wages is temporary total disability benefits. These benefits occur when an employee is taken totally out of work by his doctor. A worker is entitled to two-thirds of his pre-injury average weekly wage for a maximum of 500

weeks (91/2 years). This does not mean you will get automatically receive the full 500 weeks. What it means is, if the doctor keeps you out of work up to 500 weeks, you will be able to receive two-thirds of your average weekly wage. What the doctor says goes.

It does not matter if the insurance adjuster thinks you can work or if you believe you cannot work, the doctor determines whether or not you can be deemed totally out of work. Being totally out of work means you are not capable of doing any work. It is much more than not being able to go back to your old job. The amount you are owed is based on what is called your "average weekly wage." The average weekly

wage is determined by the last 52 weeks of employment. It includes bonuses, overtime, uniforms, meals, etc.

On July 1, 2015, the maximum weekly compensation rate was $975.00. This means that if your average weekly wage is over $1,462.50 (or any amount higher than $1,462.60), you will only get $975.00 per week and not 2/3rds of your average weekly wage.

There is also a minimum compensation rate, which, as of July 1, 2015, was $243.75. This means that, if your average weekly wage is between $365.62 and $243.75, your compensation rate will be the minimum compensation rate of $243.75 rather than 2/3rds . However, if your average weekly wage is less than

$243.75, your compensation rate will be the same as your average weekly wage.

Temporary total disability starts when an employee has been out of work for at least seven days. Once an employee is out of work for 21 days, he will also be reimbursed for the first seven days as well. There are many pitfalls with temporary total disability. In general, for most injuries, 91/2 years will be sufficient time. The unfortunate event occurs when an individual may never return to work and 91/2 years will definitely not be a sufficient amount of time to get lost wages.

You are also entitled to receive cost of living adjustments (COLA) each year with temporary total disability. This might seem like a small amount of money. However, I was contacted by an individual who had been on workers' compensation for eight years and had never received COLA. When she did get her past years' cost of living adjustments, it was over $20,000. That was money she could have used to make ends meet during that time frame, but since she had never asked, the insurance adjuster never told her about it, and she did not receive her cost of living adjustments. Sometimes, the amount even surprises me. In another case, my client came to me and was on workers' compensation and Social Security Disability (a huge mess in and of itself that I will not address now). When you are receiving Social Security Disability and temporary total disability, you cannot get a cost of living adjustment from workers' compensation. However, there had been a few years in the past before she was on Social Security and we thought at least we can get her a little bit of money. The benefits to which she was entitled totaled $13,000.00, just for her cost of living adjustment.

As I stated, you can't get a cost of living increase for your workers' comp benefits if you're also on Social Security Disability. Technically, the theory is that you get the cost of living increase from Social Security and so there is no "double dipping." However, even though you cannot receive a cost of living adjustment while on Social Security Disability ; when you turn age 65, your Social Security Disability turns into a Social Security Retirement , and then you can get a cost of living increase on your workers' comp check again. In general, I still don't like people being on both Social Security Disability and workers' comp because, among other complications, Social Security Disability makes your workers' comp check taxable. However, this is a way for folks in these situations to get a little extra money coming in when they turn 65 and their Social Security Disability benefits convert to Social Security Retirement benefits.

The point is, you just never know. In the appendix, I have a cost of living adjustment form for your use. You can go to my website and download the form at **www. injuredworkerslawfirm.com**. Social Security gives cost of living adjustments also, so you would not get both a workers' compensation cost of living adjustment and a Social Security Disability cost of living adjustment.

The other type of lost wage benefit is temporary partial disability. You can get this if the doctor says you can work light duty and you actually return to work, but you are not able to make the amount of money that you were making before the injury, you will get 2/3rds of the difference between your pre-injury average weekly wage and your post injury wage. Neither Cost of living adjustments nor minimum compensation rates apply to temporary partial disability, but the maximum compensation rate does. This means that, even after you return work with restrictions, if your wage loss is greater than $1,462.50, you will only receive $975.00.

2. **Medical benefits for your injury.** The employee is entitled to lifetime medical benefits as long as the treatment is related to the original work injury and the treatment is deemed reasonable and necessary by the treating physician. To get a treating physician, your employer must provide you with a panel of at least three physicians from three different practices from which to choose. If they do not provide you a panel within a reasonable period of time or your employer denies your workers' compensation claim, you can choose your own treating physician. It is horrible that a valid claim may be denied, but the silver lining is that you get to choose your own treating physician. Many unscrupulous insurance adjusters put physicians

on their panels that they hope will be more in favor of the employer and the insurance company than the injured worker. The issue of providing a panel within a "reasonable time" is very difficult to figure out and really just depends on the severity of the injury. Many times employers and insurance companies deny medical benefits, saying that the medical treatment is not related to the accident. This happens often with back injuries. Many times, people may have had sore backs prior to a significant accident at work. The insurance company may try to say that the recommended back surgery is due to these prior minor injuries and not due to the current work accident. It is important to know that significant aggravations of pre-existing conditions are covered under workers' compensation. This means that even though you may have prior back issues, if you have an accident at work that aggravates your back, you will be able to get medical treatment for it. The problem comes with employers and insurance companies trying to say that the accident was not significant enough to cause any aggravation to your prior injuries. Therefore, it is very important when you talk to the physician to make sure you are very clear with him so your injury is documented correctly. Medical benefits include all medical treatment for the injury. This includes prescriptions, mileage, and medical equipment. There are no co-payments. You are entitled to mileage to and from physical therapy, to and from the doctor, to and from hospitals for diagnostic tests, and any medical treatment. As of 2015, mileage is 55.5 cents per mile. In the appendix, I have attached a sample mileage chart to help you collect your mileage benefits. You can go to my website and download the form at **www. injuredworkerslawfirm.com**.

3. **Loss of use of a body part.** The legal term is permanent partial disability benefits. When an employee permanently loses the use or partial use of certain body parts that are specifically listed in the Virginia Workers Compensation Act, he is entitled to permanent partial disability benefits. The neck itself and the back itself are not covered; however, many times a back injury will cause problems to legs, or a neck injury may cause problems with arms. Then, you would be entitled to a disability rating to those body parts. As I said before, there is no money for pain and suffering, but this benefit is somewhat like getting reimbursed for pain and suffering since you are being compensated for the permanent loss of range of motion, among other things. The amount you are given is calculated by a standard math formula. It is the percentage rating your doctor gives you for the loss of use of the body part member, multiplied by the number of weeks for that body part, multiplied by two-thirds of your average weekly wage. In the appendix, I have attached the number of weeks for each body part. You can go to my website and download the form at **www.injuredworkerslawfirm. com**. As an example, let's say you have a 10 percent

loss of use of your right leg due to a knee injury and before the accident you made $1,000 a week. The formula would be: .10 x 175 weeks x $666.67, which equals $11,666.73. Several things must occur before you can get permanent partial disability benefits. First, your doctor has to say that you've reached maximum medical improvement. This basically means that there is nothing more he can do for you and you're not going to get significantly better than you already are as of that date. The next thing is that your workers' compensation treating physician has to give a disability rating to the body part lost. Usually, this is done by the doctor referring you to a physical therapist to have a Functional Capacity Evaluation (FCE). Once the FCE has been completed and the physical therapist drafts the report, it is submitted to your doctor, who either approves or changes the rating that the physical therapist has given. Next, the insurance company needs to agree that the appropriate rating and agreement form will be created for your signature in order for you to receive your benefits. These benefits will be paid weekly, just as your temporary total disability benefit check. You cannot receive a temporary total (lost wages) check and a permanent partial disability check at the same time. Thus, what normally happens is that the employee is either released to full duty or returns to work, which stops the temporary total check, and at that point he would begin receiving his weekly checks of permanent partial disability benefits. If requested, the employee can ask the insurance adjuster for the permanent partial disability benefits in a lump sum. However, be forewarned, this is done at a cost. Usually, insurance adjusters request a 10 percent discount to give you your permanent partial disability benefits in one lump sum. I normally do not recommend my clients agree to this. Many times you may receive your workers' compensation check in a lump sum anyway, simply due to the passage of time trying to get the paperwork straight. In the above example, if paid weekly, it would only be 17 1/2 weeks (4 months). I do not think it is worth $1,166.67 to get the money within the month versus spread over four months. If you are receiving temporary partial disability benefits, you may request the Commission to get your permanent partial disability benefits at the same time. You cannot receive a cost of living adjustment for permanent partial disability benefits.

4. **Vocational rehabilitation.** Once the doctor states that you may return to some form of light duty work, the insurance company may begin vocational rehabilitation. There are two goals of vocational rehabilitation. The first goal is to restore the employee to some form of employment and the second goal is to relieve the employer's burden of future compensation. The goal is never to find the employee a meaningful job, a convenient job, or a job that he would want. It is not an opportunity to go to college or learn a

new trade. It is solely to save the insurance company money. Vocational rehabilitation is not a benefit to the employee butrather a benefit to the insurance company. It is usually better for employees to find their own employment. The Virginia Workers' Compensation Commission's vocational guidelines are in the appendix. You can go to my website and download the form at **www. injuredworkerslawfirm. com**. If you think the vocational rehabilitation specialist is violating the rules, give him or her a copy of the guidelines and ask for an explanation.

Vocational Rehabilitation was probably originally supposed to be a benefit to the injured worker, but something happened along the way, as it is the number one threat insurance adjusters use to force a lower settlement. It is a very real and dangerous threat — depending upon how unscrupulous the rehabilitation counselor decides to act. The threat has nothing to do with the injured worker not wanting to work or not cooperating with the counselor. It has to do with insurance company lobbyists influencing the state legislature. A law created by the state legislature states if there is an allegation that the worker is not cooperating, then the insurance company can immediately stop paying and file the paperwork to terminate benefits. Just an allegation and your weekly check immediately stops! Don't they have to prove it? Don't I get a hearing? Yes, but you are without a check for six months before you get a hearing to prove you are cooperating (and longer if they appeal). The insurance adjuster will try to force a settlement by telling the injured worker that, if you do not take this low settlement, I will find a vocation rehabilitation counselor who will say you are not cooperating and see how you like having no money for six months.

5. **Death benefits.** If an employee dies as a result of his job, his dependents may be entitled to funeral expenses and two-thirds of his average weekly wage up to 500 weeks. If there are multiple dependents, such as a wife and children, the weekly benefit is divided equally. If the widower or widow remarries, then his/her benefits are terminated. When a child turns 18, his or her benefits may be terminated. Before these events occur, it may be best to talk to an attorney to discuss settlement options.

6. **Lifetime benefits.** In some very serious situations, an injured worker may be able to get permanent total disability benefits. The employee must have permanently lost the use of two extremities, whether it is hands, arms, feet, legs, eyes, or a combination thereof, or suffered any injury that results in total paralysis or a brain injury which is so severe that it leaves the employee permanently unable to find gainful employment. Some attorneys may be able to get an injured worker lifetime benefits in situations

that are not so obvious, so always ask to see if it may be a possibility for you.

CHAPTER 2

Settlements and Other Lump Sum Benefits

Whether your case is contested or uncontested, there may come a time when it is in your best interest to settle your workers' compensation claim. There are many reasons why you may desire to settle: the risk of litigation, to avoid having to deal with the insurance carrier, the desire to manage your own medical treatment, or the need for a lump sum of money. It is very important to know that neither you nor the insurance carrier can force the other side to accept a settlement. All settlements must be approved by the Virginia Workers' Compensation Commission. The Commission will only approve a settlement if it is in their opinion that it is in the best interest of the employee. It has been said (I have seen it) that injured workers get more money in a lump sum settlement when they hire an attorney as opposed to not hiring an attorney. I would, again, advise consulting with an attorney to see whether you should have an attorney help you evaluate your case and to negotiate a good settlement.

When you settle, you are usually giving up all your rights to future lost wages and future medical benefits, so it is a very serious decision that needs to be looked at from various points of view to make sure that you are making the right decision. The way cases are valued depends on how much temporary total disability benefits and permanent partial disability benefits are remaining out of the 500 weeks, what is anticipated to be the future medical services and the cost of such future medical services, and, if the matter is contested, the risk of litigation and losing at a hearing. Also, Medicare, Social Security, child support, and Medicaid may have liens on the settlement money. Medicare even goes so far as to say it has an interest in the workers' compensation settlement if there is a reasonable expectation if you might receive Medicare within 30 months after settling your workers' compensation claim and the settlement is greater than $250,000. Again, these issues need to be discussed at length with your attorney to figure out how to maximize your benefits. Always remember, the insurance companies are looking out for the insurance company , not you. The standard attorney fee for settlements is 20 percent.

Some people mistakenly believe they should not settle because they can get a much bigger verdict going to a hearing. This is not the case at all. Workers' compensation is a pay-as-you-go system. The Workers' Compensation Commission does not have the power to grant a lump sum award. There is no jury trial. The Commission only has the power to rule that you are or that you are not entitled to benefits (a weekly check, medical care, etc.).

If your case has been accepted and the insurance company is doing what they are legally required to do, you will never go to a hearing.

Other Benefits, Liens, And How They Affect Your Workers' Compensation Benefits

What about other benefits besides workers' compensation? It is beyond this guidebook to discuss all the other types of benefits. However, because workers' compensation benefits are limited, it is very important to know how they coordinate with other benefits and if you may be able to get benefits from another source, as well as workers' compensation benefits.

1. **The biggest sum for an individual would come from what is called a third-party personal injury claim.** An injured worker cannot sue his employer. He can only file a workers' compensation claim against his employer. However, there may be a "3rd" person who was negligent, causing your injury. Here are some examples: A medical malpractice claim against the treating physician, a personal injury claim against a non-coworker for an auto accident, equipment maintenance, delivery of materials, or premise liability. Another type is products liability, which would be a claim against a manufacturer for defective equipment. If you believe there may be a possibility that the equipment that you were using (such as a forklift or a table saw) was defective, it is important to preserve

that evidence by taking pictures or, ideally, by keeping the equipment so it cannot be destroyed and having an expert look at it. The reason these types of cases are "better" than a workers' compensation case is because you can get money for pain and suffering. As you recall, in workers' compensation, you can only get a portion of lost wages for up to 9 1/2 years plus medical benefits under workers' compensation. This is not enough if you have a significant life-changing injury where you may never be able to go back to your career. You may have permanent disabilities and, physically, cannot do various daily living activities that you used to do. These are not compensated under workers' compensation; however, in third party claims, you can get what is called pain and suffering and you would be able to be compensated for those types of losses.

Workers' compensation has a lien on any personal injury claim that you pursue, so, if the workers compensation insurance company has paid any money to you or for medical treatment on your behalf, you will have to pay them back. If you chose not to pursue a third party claim, the workers' compensation insurance company may do it anyway in your place. For this reason, if you settle your third party case, it is very important that you get permission from the workers compensation insurance company to settle the third party case

Usually, the workers compensation insurance company will agree to waive or reduce their lien if the employee settles the workers' compensation claim as well. If the employee settles a third party personal injury claim without the knowledge and consent of the employer or workers' compensation insurance carrier, he will forfeits his right to further workers' compensation benefits, including lost wages, loss of use, and medical benefits

2. **Medicaid has a lien for the total amount paid by Medicaid on the workers' compensation claim.** If you have used Medicaid to pay for any medical treatment that should have been paid by the workers compensation carrier, Medicaid wants to be paid back.

3. **Social Security disability is offset by the amount of workers' compensation benefits the injured worker receives.** As I mentioned before, I had an elderly individual come into my office who had settled his workers' compensation claim for $75,000, for which he was very proud, since he had done it on his own. Unfortunately, the settlement paperwork had no language in it protecting his Social Security disability benefits. Therefore, when he was awarded Social Security disability benefits after his settlement, for which he was supposed to get $800 a month, he only received approximately $200 a month for the next 5 1/2 years because he had settled his workers' compensation claim without the correct language protecting him in

the settlement papers. At the end of that 5 1/2 year period, he will go back up to the $800 in Social Security disability benefits but what has happened, in effect, is he has settled his workers' compensation case for nothing because Social Security took 100 percent credit for the $75,000 until, in essence, that lump sum had been used up. What should have happened is that the lump sum settlement should have been apportioned over the individual's lifetime. When it is apportioned, many times there is no reduction in the claimant's Social Security disability benefits or at a minimum only about $10-$20 per month.

4. **Medicare is very involved in workers' compensation claims.** The federal government does not want to pay for any medical treatment which is the responsibility of the workers' compensation insurance company . Therefore, Medicare is prohibited from paying for medical services that have been or can reasonably be expected to be paid under workers' compensation. If Medicare mistakenly pays for a claim, then Medicare has a lien. It has the right to recover 100 percent of its payments. This is one reason why it is very important that your medical treatment is paid through the workers' compensation insurance carrier and not your regular health insurance and definitely not through Medicare or Medicaid. This prevents Medicare from having a lien on any future settlement that you may have. If you are planning on settling your workers'

compensation claim, Medicare may have an interest regarding the funds that have been allocated towards future medical treatment. All parties are supposed to protect Medicare's interests in any settlement. In many cases, Medicare's written approval is required before you settle your workers' compensation claim. The criteria and financial guidelines are subject to change by Medicare. Medicare has regulations and issues internal memorandums that give guidance to individuals on how to deal with Medicare, and I suggest you go to their website for the most up-to-date criteria.

5. **There is also short term and long term disability payments.** Many employers have private insurance policies that exclude workers' compensation benefits, however, if your case is contested you may be able to get short term and long term disability benefits during the pendency of fighting your workers' compensation claim. When you prevail at the workers' compensation hearing, your employer will get credit for all short term and long term disability payments they made. In a recent case, I settled the workers' compensation case and by carefully, honestly, drafting the settlement documents and other conditions for the settlement, my client received his lump sum workers' compensation settlement and was allowed to go on long term disability. The best of both worlds!

6. **State Unemployment Benefits.** If you can't work at all, then you are not entitled to receive unemployment

benefits. However, if your workers' compensation claim has been denied and you have light duty restrictions, you may be able to get unemployment benefits. If you have been laid off or your employer is not going to accommodate your light duty restrictions, then you may file for unemployment. However, if your claim is contested and you eventually do win or receive workers' compensation benefits down the road for the same period for which you received unemployment benefits, you will have to pay the unemployment benefits back to the Virginia Employment Commission.

CHAPTER 3

The Most Important Legal Issues That Can Cause Problems With Your Workers' Compensation Claim

Workers' compensation is a "No-Fault" remedy created by statute. Negligence on the part of the employer or a co-employee is not an issue. Workers' compensation statutes and case law have changed the nature of workers' compensation and have carved out many exceptions. There are numerous written materials on the legal issues surrounding workers' compensation and it is beyond the scope of this guidebook to provide a detailed analysis. However, since knowledge is power, I think it is important for you to know the more common issues to help you understand your workers' compensation claim. The injured worker has the burden to prove each element of his injury by accident. He must prove that he had an injury by accident that arose out of and in the course of his employment, which resulted in incapacity.

What Is "An Injury By Accident"?

First, you must prove an injury by accident. This may seem simple but it is probably one of the most common reasons why workers' compensation claims are denied. To prove an injury by accident, the injured worker must prove a SPECIFIC IDENTIFIABLE INCIDENT that occurred at a reasonably definite time, which is the cause of an obvious sudden mechanical or structural change in the body. This is the legal definition. It basically means that you have to prove that your accident happened suddenly, at a specific time, while you were performing a specific work-related task. Gradual injuries or injuries sustained at an unknown time are not covered. Here is an example of a gradual injury: You are a painter and lift ten buckets of paint and put them in the back of your truck. At the end of lifting the buckets, you feel pain in your back and have a herniated disc. THIS WOULD NOT BE COVERED UNDER WORKERS' COMPENSATION. However, if you were putting the buckets of paint in the truck and, as you were putting the third bucket in the bed of the truck, you felt a pull or pain in your lower back and continued working, it would be covered under workers' compensation because you would be able to specifically say as you were putting the third bucket in, you felt a sharp pain, pull, pop, etc. Proving an injury by accident is one of the top reasons you may want to hire a workers' compensation attorney.

What Is "Arising Out Of Employment"?

This means that there needs to be a connection between your injury and the conditions of your work. Here is an example. You are walking up or down normal steps at work and your knee gives way and you fall. This does not arise out of employment and would not be covered under workers' compensation. In general, if you fall and you don't know why, then it will not be covered under workers' compensation. However, if you slipped due to oil on the floor or because you were carrying a box that caused you to miss a step on the stairwell, it would be covered. Many people who slip and fall at work are denied workers' compensation because they are not paying attention to the exact reason why they fell because they don't think that it matters. It is very important to remember what caused your fall, that it was related to your work conditions, and that you tell people the *cause* of the fall, not just that you fell.

What If I Get A Disease From Work?

Though the most common types of injuries covered under workers' compensation are accidents, occupational diseases are also covered. An occupational disease is considered a disease that arises out of and in the course of employment (just like accident requirements) and it's not an ordinary disease of life, which you are exposed to outside of employment. Some examples of diseases that could be considered occupational diseases are AIDS and HIV, asthma, allergic reactions, heart attacks, or cancer. Some diseases that are consideredordinary diseases of life may also be compensable under workers' compensation. Some ordinary diseases of life, such as hearing loss and carpal tunnel syndrome, could be covered under workers' compensation if it is established by clear and convincing evidence to a reasonable degree of medical certainty that it arose out of and was in the course of employment. It cannot result from outside causes of employment. This is a higher burden of proof than just by a preponderance of the evidence. It is kind of like saying, instead of proving by 51%, you have to prove it by 75%. There are some special rules regarding occupational diseases that are a little bit different than injuries by accident. For example, unlike pre-existing conditions with injuries by accident, if a disease is already in existence prior to the exposure at employment, it is not covered under workers' compensation, even if work aggravated it. An example would be asthma: paint fumes in the work place aggravate your pre-existing asthma so that you no longer can work. This would not be covered. However, if you'd never had asthma before and the paint fumes caused the asthma, then it could be covered under workers' compensation. The date that an injured worker is told that he or she has an occupational disease and that it was caused by work is considered the date of accident for purposes of obtaining workers' compensation benefits with occupational diseases. This usually is a medical question that needs to be adequately documented by your doctor in your medical records.

Here Are More Ways The Insurance Company Will Try To Deny Your Valid Claim

Statute of Limitations. As stated earlier, injured workers have the burden to prove several things before they are entitled to receive workers' compensation benefits. There are a few common defenses that insurance companies bring up to which you need to pay special attention. One is the statute of limitations. An injury by accident claim needs to be filed with the Virginia Workers' Compensation Commission within two years of the date of the accident. Many times, an injured worker is caught unaware because the insurance company voluntarily makes payments for two years, and after two years when their checks stop arriving, they realize that they were supposed to file a claim for benefits with the Virginia Workers' Compensation Commission and the statute of limitations has run. There is very little wiggle room. You can't keep getting benefits just because you didn't know that you were supposed to file a claim. Also, if you're filing for permanent partial disability benefits, also known as a loss of use rating, it must be filed within three years from the date you were last paid workers' compensation benefits pursuant to an award. If you have already received an Award, and you want to file a change in condition (for example: you've gone back to work and now a second surgery is required and you need to go back out of work), you need to file with the Virginia Workers' Compensation Commission within two years from the date that compensation was last paid pursuant to an Award Order. Here is an example: you were paid lost wages pursuant to an Award Order that ended January 1, 2006 and then on January

1, 2007, your doctor took you back out of work for one year; the insurance company paid you voluntarily without an Award Order and you never filed or notified the Virginia Workers' Compensation Commission; then as of January 1, 2008, if you are taken out of work again, you would not get any lost wages because the statute of limitations ran. However, if an Award Order had been entered for the timeframe between January 2007 and January 2008, you would still have until January 2010 before the two-year statute of limitations would be finished. Some of the statutes of limitation can be confusing. The most important thing you need to remember is that every time you get workers' compensation benefits, you need to make sure that agreements forms are sent to you by the insurance company for your signature and that they are forwarded to the Virginia Workers' Compensation Commission for entry of an Award Order. If you are not sent agreement forms, you need to file a claim for benefits. This is the best way of protecting yourself from the pitfalls of too much time elapsing and being taken advantage of by the insurance company. If in doubt, call our office to be certain you are doing everything within the right timelines.

Notice

The employee must notify the employer of the accident within 30 days of the accident. If you fail to do this, your claim *may* be denied. Obviously, the ideal situation is to notify your employer immediately and in writing. Some employers have rules that injuries need to be reported within 24 hours. If you don't make your employer's deadline, you don't forfeit your workers' compensation benefits but the insurance adjuster will deny your claim and make you fight for your benefits.

Willful Misconduct—Or Insurance Companies Looking For Loopholes

If an employee is hurt due to "willful misconduct," his claim may be lost. It makes sense, but the insurance company will grab on to anything to deny a claim. If you are drunk at work and are hurt, of course your claim should be denied. But, what if you were going one mile over the speed limit or you don't recall your speed, then you are in a car wreck and you are now paralyzed? Examples of willful misconduct would be: intoxication, incarceration, violating a statutory rule such as speeding or reckless driving, or violating a work safety rule. The law for work safety rules is that the employer has to show that the rule was reasonable, it was known to the injured worker, it was for the injured worker's benefit, and the worker intentionally undertook the forbidden act. I've seen some tragic events occur to individuals under this rule. Many times, employers have safety rules but they are not followed. It can be hard to prove that no one obeys the safety rules. My best advice is to follow all work safety rules as closely as possible, but at the same time remember that just because your employer is saying you violated a safety rule does not mean that if you fight it, you won't win your benefits.

Insurance companies also try to deny workers' compensation claims alleging an injured worker misrepresented something on an employment application. The law is that it must be a significant misrepresentation that they relied on and there has to be a relationship between the misrepresentation and the injury. So, for example, if you have a bad back and you failed to disclose your bad back on your application and then broke your foot at work, it would not matter. However, if you injured your back, it could bar you from receiving workers' compensation benefits.

Insurance companies also try to set you up to "refuse" certain workers' compensation requirements in order to deny your benefits. One example is "refusal of employment." If your employer has found you a job for you that your doctor says you can do, you must take it or benefits are cut off. Failure to cooperate with your vocational rehabilitation specialist, to include refusing to meet with that person or not following up with phone calls and failure to look for light duty employment are other examples of refusal. This is a very frustrating situation for many of my clients who want control or choice over job placements. The law is that when you have been released to light duty work, you are supposed to make a good faith effort to find employment within your capabilities. However, it does not mean going back to your old job. If you've had the same job as a plumber for 25 years, it's very difficult to comprehend that if your doctor says you can drive, you need to be looking for taxicab employment. It can be stressful if you've always been a daycare provider or you've always done heavy labor and the insurance company wants you at a desk job, answering the phone. Unfortunately, it is very, very important to document your employment search because this is a very common trick that is used to try to cut individual workers' benefits off. See the appendix for job search guidelines and a chart to help you.

"Refusing medical treatment" is another pitfall. This does not occur very often but it may occur when a doctor is recommending surgery and the injured worker really does not want to have surgery. It can occur if you miss doctor appointments or physical therapy appointments. Also, a doctor's comment to get your blood pressure under control and you not following up with your family doctor may give the insurance company an excuse to cut off your benefits. There are ways to get around this type of situation and it would be best to speak to a lawyer about how to best strategize so that you cannot be labeled as refusing medical treatment which would cause your checks and medical treatment to be cut off.

CHAPTER 4

Steps To Follow With A Workers' Compensation Claim

First, immediately report your injury to your employer even if you do not believe you need medical treatment. Next, file a claim for benefits. If your employer has done what they are supposed to do after you report your injury, your employer notifies its workers' compensation carrier than an injury has occurred. The workers' compensation carrier then files a First Report of Injury with the Virginia Workers' Compensation Commission. This tells the Commission that an injury has been reported. These filings are usually done electronically. The workers' compensation carrier will then call you to get a tape-recorded statement as to what occurred and to attempt to make a decision whether or not to accept your claim. The recorded statement is the insurance adjuster's opportunity to find any grounds to deny your claim. I usually advise my clients not to give a recorded statement because there are certain things that they could be led into answering that could destroy their case. However, sometimes, to speed the process along, it could be an option to give your recorded statement quickly. You would need to speak to a lawyer to get advice as to which would be the best option for you, given the circumstances that you are in at the time. Assuming that the insurance adjuster accepts your claim, they usually begin making voluntary payments of two-thirds of your average weekly wage within a few weeks and they will give you a panel of physicians for you to pick one to become your workers' compensation treating physician. Many times, the insurance company continues to make voluntary payments but does not file the First Report of Injury with the Virginia Workers' Compensation Commission. At this point, it's important to note that if you have not received a claim for benefits form from the Workers' Compensation Commission, you should request one; either online or in person at the Commission. A sample copy is in the appendix. You can go to my website and download the form at **www.injuredworkerslawfirm.com**. Filing this claim for benefits is very important. At that point, the Virginia Workers' Compensation Commission generates documents to the insurance carrier that are called the 20 Day Order-Claim Filed.. This 20 Day Order is a form that the insurance adjuster has to return to the Virginia Workers' Compensation Commission within 20 days advising the Commission whether they are sending agreement forms, and if not, why they are denying the claim. . You would then get a copy of this document. A 20-Day Order will also be sent when the workers' compensation carrier notifies the Commission that payments have been made. This is called a 20-Day Order-Payments Made. When you receive the response to this form, read the response carefully, as it may tell you that agreement forms are not being sent because no claim has been filed. If this is the case, file a claim for benefits immediately.

If the workers' compensation carrier accepts the claim for lost wages, an Award Order would be entered. This is the document that you are looking for when there is any change in your case. You want Award Orders entered so that you're under what's called an Open Award, as opposed to not having an Award and the employer just making voluntary payments. This is important for several reasons. One reason is that if you're being voluntarily paid with no Award Order and a conflict comes up six months to a year later, you will still have to prove the injury by accident occurred. Many witnesses may be gone and, at the very least, their memories have faded. The conflict may be whether or not you should have surgery and now you also have to fight and prove whether an actual accident occurred. Once an Order is entered, the insurance company is legally responsible for that injury by accident and you would never have to go back and try to prove the injury occurred. The second reason why Award Orders are so important is, once you're under an Award Order you can ask, under some circumstances, for an expedited hearing if an issue arises. This would mean you would have your hearing more quickly than waiting with all the other individuals whose claims are being denied. Usually, this would cut the time before your case is heard by three to four months. Cutting the litigation time by three of four months, during which time the insurance company is not paying you, , may mean a lot to you financially. Don't forget that your bills, like electric, rent, and mortgage are not going to go away because you are hurt on the job. You must be proactive and get your Award Orders to prevent such a financial disaster before there is any conflict. Also, if the insurance company is more than 14 days late with your check, they have to pay you extra money when there is an Award Order (and they don't have to if you don't have an Award Order).

The Virginia Workers' Commission, as of 10/1/08, changed several forms and processes. For any accident after 10/1/08, the form names have been changed to the First Report of Injury (FROI) and then a Subsequent Report of Injury (SROI). However, older forms may still be used, so you may see two different types of paperwork. They will be treated the same. The most important thing is that you put the correct body part injured on each and every document. If you state only "neck" and it's also your shoulder, the insurance company only has to cover the neck.

If the insurance company has denied your claim, Part B at the bottom half of your claim for benefits form would need to be completed to get a hearing scheduled. Usually, it will be another four to five months before you have the hearing date. The Deputy Commissioner does not make a decision at the hearing. He will listen to the evidence and then render a written opinion that you will receive in the mail a few weeks later. After the decision has been made, either party has 30 days to note an appeal of that opinion. If an appeal if filed, then the Full Commission will look at the evidence presented in the original hearing and make a decision. (You will not need to testify again on the same issues) After the Full Commission's decision, either party has 30 days to note an appeal of this opinion to the Virginia Court of Appeals. As you can see, this process can be very long. If your claim is denied, consult an attorney. You will have experts in workers' compensation fighting against you. The insurance adjuster, who does this work full time, will hire a defense attorney who usually does this type of work full time. Therefore, it usually is advisable at least to consult with an attorney if your claim is being denied, to know whether you have a claim, and to explain the legal processes to you.

I would estimate that out of ten people who are denied workers' compensation benefits and come to me to discuss their denials, four will clearly have a case, three probably do, and three do not. Another reason to get an attorney if your claim is denied is that the hearing process needs to be done correctly and proper legal procedures need to be followed. The hearing is your one and only opportunity to put on evidence. You cannot say, "Oh, I can get that to you later." While you're waiting for your hearing, you will have what is legally called a discovery period. You will be filing medical records. Each party will ask the other written questions, called "interrogatories" which must be answered under oath. You or your treating physician may be asked verbal questions in a proceeding called a "deposition". Usually, at a deposition you would go to your attorney's office and the insurance company's attorney would ask you questions under oath in front of a court reporter. Make no mistake, your answers will be used against you at your hearing. Usually, a hearing is set for 30 minutes. Most of the time, if you hire an attorney you will be responsible for the attorney's fees. However, if there is no reasonable defense at all, sometimes the Commission may assess attorney's fees against the insurance company.

CHAPTER 5

How Best To Deal With Nurse Case Managers

A nurse case manager may be assigned to your case. The role of the nurse case manager is to monitor your care and report back to the insurance adjuster. Many times, the nurse may put pressure on the doctor to force an injured worker back to work too quickly or to suggest cheaper medical treatment as opposed to what a physician may truly want to do. Never forget who is paying the nurse case manager and that they have an agenda to save the insurance company money. Many times, a nurse case manager can convince a doctor to release an injured worker back to work even if the doctor had not originally intended to do so. Other times, they may recommend to the insurance company to deny the recommended treatment because, in their opinion, they don't feel that it's necessary. Although there are many good nurse case managers out there with a genuine desire to help, many times it appears they are more interested in helping the carrier and employer. A good nurse case manager getsmedical procedures requested by your doctor approved quickly by the insurance adjuster and helps coordinate your care if you have several medical specialists.

Here Is A Case In Point That Has Happened To More Than One Of My Clients:

They leave an appointment with the nurse case manager still there with the doctor, and get a call the next day from their employer saying they are fired because they didn't show up for work and that the doctor had released them to full duty. The nurse case manager got the doctor to "adjust" the work restrictions, gave it to the employer, and "forgot" to inform the injured worker. Don't forget, the nurse case manager is working for the insurance company. Following are tips to help you deal with your nurse case manager.

1. **Always insist upon a private examination by your doctor outside the presence of the nurse case manager.** You have the right to a private examination with your physician. This will give you an opportunity to discuss your medical issues privately with your doctor. If the nurse case manager walks into the room, you simply ask the doctor if there could be some privacy during your meeting with him and, hopefully, that will do the trick and he will ask the nurse case manager to leave and come back at the end of the appointment. A second part of this is to try to avoid having the nurse case manager talking privately with your physician by

staying present until the end of the appointment. Don't leave the doctor's office unless the nurse case manager is with you or leaves at the same time. If the nurse case manager asks to speak to the doctor privately, you should ask to join in that conversation.

2. **Never let the nurse case manager switch your treating physician without your consent.** One of the greatest areas of abuse in the workers' compensation system is the habit of "doctor shopping," especially when the insurance adjuster does not like the authorized treating physician's opinion (usually regarding work restrictions or the capacity to work). A trick I have seen a few times is the nurse case manager says the doctor you picked is not available for a month or more and you could see another particular doctor this week. There is a reason why one doctor is booked and the other is not. Why would anyone go to a doctor who has no patients? My suggestion is to set the appointment for next month and tell the receptionist to call you if there are any cancellations so you could come in immediately. Unfortunately, there are a few doctors to whom the insurance companies always send injured workers for second opinions, or treatment, or Independent Medical Examinations when they want an opinion that the worker is able to return to work without restrictions or with very little restrictions. A lawyer who handles workers' compensation cases on a regular basis knows who these doctors are and knows what they're going to

say even before the worker has been seen by the doctor. The insurance industry knows these doctors will be a great value to them for the money they are being paid and will make every effort to be sure that the injured worker is seen by those doctors. These very few doctors are paid hundreds of thousands of dollars each year by insurance companies to do their dirty work.

3. **Keep your lawyer informed.** You need to keep your lawyer informed of any significant discussions that you may have with your nurse case manager. It is essential for you to keep your lawyer informed if you feel that your nurse case manager is taking a position contrary to your interests or is working against you in obvious ways. Any concerns that you have with your nurse case manager should be discussed with your attorney.

CHAPTER 6

How Best To Deal With Doctors Who Treat You

I cannot overstress the importance of the role of your workers' compensation treating physician in your case. Besides the fact he will be one who will be taking care of your physical needs, his opinions will decide the legal consequences of your workers' compensation claim. Therefore, it's very important to have a good relationship with your workers' compensation treating physician even if this physician has been chosen by the insurance company. Since your workers' compensation treating physician's opinion is given great weight when an issue arises about what *caused* a medical problem or if a particular treatment may be reasonable and necessary, his opinion is very important. Here are some tips when dealing with your doctor:

1. **Describe the work accident specifically on the first visit to the doctor.** One of the worst mistakes that an injured worker can make is not to describe in detail

on his or her first visit to the doctor the facts of the accident. It is difficult to prove that you had an injury by accident if in the first doctor's visit there are no notes in the history section as to how the injury occurred. Therefore, it is very important to state to the doctor where you were and what occurred. Then, in his notes, in the history section (which is in all medical notes) it will state "slipped and fell at work" or "lifted a box at work." You need to understand that there is no doctor/patient privilege in workers' compensation. Thus, all your medical records will be read by the insurance adjuster and can also be read by the insurance defense attorney and the Virginia Workers' Compensation Commission. (Unfortunately, this includes medical records not related to your work injury, or for treatment that happened before your work injury.) Therefore, it's also important not to make statements to the doctor that you would not want other individuals to know. Of course, be truthful with your doctor so he can treat you as effectively as possible but avoid getting into arguments with your physician or rambling about non-work related medical conditions unless you do not mind the insurance company knowing.

2. **Talk to your doctor about your job duties and your work restrictions.** If at all possible, try to get the doctor to discuss with you your pre-injury job duties and his opinion about your return to work restrictions, your functional capacity, and anything related to your ability

to return to work before he gives them to the insurance company. Many times, a nurse case manager may try to unfairly influence the doctor's opinion with regard to these issues. Thus, if you bring up this issue with your doctor first, you would at least have an opportunity to present your views to the doctor on an equal basis with the nurse case manager.

Always mention all body parts that were injured. Every time, especially the first time, you go to the doctor it is important that you reiterate every body part that has been injured as a result of the work accident. If a body part is not mentioned, it will be cause for the insurance company to deny treatment in the future for that injured body part. Many insurance adjusters will deny medical treatment for a body part not mentioned in the first appointment. I have had to help injured workers get medical treatment for serious injuries to the neck that did not get mentioned until the second doctor visit because the pain in the shoulder was so severe that the neck problem didn't seem that important. Therefore, if you have one area that hurts really badly and one area that hurts a little bit, you still need to tell the doctor about *both*.

Always get a disability slip stating what you physically can and cannot do from your doctor. Before you leave your doctor's office, always get a disability slip. The workers' compensation insurance company is not going to pay you a weekly check unless they have a copy of a disability slip that says you are not able to work or your work restrictions are such that your employer cannot accommodate the restrictions.

There are many areas of potential conflict with your doctor. Here are some scenarios that could come up:

- Your doctor may return you to work (light duty or full duty) before you feel physically ready;

- Your doctor may state your current medical problems and treatment are not related to your work accident;

- Your doctor may state there are no medical objective findings that you are injured;

- The doctor may state you are exaggerating your pain and symptoms or that you are malingering;

- Your doctor may recommend a treatment plan or surgery that you do not want to undergo.

If any of these situations come up, you need to immediately talk to a workers' compensation attorney. The worst case scenario is your medical care and weekly check are cut off. The best case scenario is to avoid the conflict with your physician with a good legal strategy.

CHAPTER 7

How Best To Deal With A Vocational Rehabilitation Counselor

Once you have permanent restrictions and you cannot go back to your former employment due to the restrictions, the insurance carrier may assign a vocational rehabilitation counselor to you. This person's sole task is to find you a job as soon as possible to save the insurance company money by cutting off your workers' compensation benefits. Their goal is not to boost your career, encourage knowledge fulfillment, self-improvement, or any find any type of job satisfaction. There is much litigation in this area due to the antagonistic situation injured workers are put into. Here are a few tips that may help you if you are in this situation.

1. **Always have your lawyer present at your first interview with the vocational rehabilitation specialist.** One of the main purposes of vocational rehabilitation counselors is to wear down the worker and harass the

worker to the extent that he or she becomes willing to settle the workers' compensation claim cheaply. They create a lot of busy work for the injured employee. Vocational rehabilitation counselors will, for instance, send workers in search of jobs that they know the workers are not qualified to perform. They will send them letters saying "I've attempted to contact you by phone several times" and, in fact, have not actually contacted you at all by phone. Hopefully, this first meeting with the lawyer will help discourage the vocation rehabilitation worker from unprofessional activities and make the vocational rehabilitation a little bit easier for the injured employee.

2. **Don't make conversation with the rehabilitation counselor. He or she is not your best friend or buddy**. As stated elsewhere in this book, one of the defenses in a workers' compensation case is that the employee refused to cooperate with the vocational rehabilitation counselor. Therefore, it's very important never to say "I'm not going to be looking for any job that doesn't pay at least $8.00 an hour," or, "I can't do any work so I'm not even going to look." Vocational rehabilitation counselors love this because they can twist it to make it appear that the worker is refusing to cooperate. The insurance company will file an application to cut off workers' compensation benefits when these types of statements are made, alleging that the worker refused to cooperate with vocational rehabilitation efforts. The

law allows them to suspend the benefits as long as the refusal to cooperate continues. As a practical matter, it is difficult to get benefits reinstated once they've been suspended for failure to comply and, at a minimum, you'd be without a check for several months until a decision by the Virginia Workers' Compensation Commission is made (assuming that the other side does not appeal). All of your actions and words should convey to the counselor that you are willing to cooperate fully and completely with any and all reasonable efforts at vocational rehabilitation.

3. **Return to work as soon as possible**. At our law firm, we always encourage injured workers to return to work as quickly as possible. You will be earning more income and you will have a more positive image of yourself when working. It helps the financial and mental health of the entire family. Also, if you *choose* your work, you are choosing your own destiny and making your own choices, as opposed to the vocational rehabilitation counselor forcing you into a job that he or she finds for you. This does not mean, however, that you should just jeopardize your health and go back to work before your doctor says that you are ready to do so. It's important to make sure that the job has been approved by your treating physician. Don't allow the vocational rehabilitation counselor to talk you into inappropriate situations. Many rehabilitation counselors try to coax a worker into saying that he is capable of doing almost

any type of work, even when the worker knows he can't. The counselor will take these statements, blow them out of proportion, and use the statements against the worker in a termination hearing. They will ask the worker such things as whether he climbs a ladder or if he can use hand tools and whether he does his own dishes or mows his own lawn. If the worker says, "No, I can't climb a ladder or use the tools," the counselor will say, "Are you sure? Aren't you willing to try?" Again, such statements will be blown out of proportion and used against you. Another thing that the vocational rehabilitation counselor may try to do is convince someone to go into business for himself. Many times, workers are lulled into settling their case for less by vocational rehabilitation counselors who convince them that they could start their own business with money that they receive from settling their workers' compensation claim. This is a very dangerous proposal and needs to be considered carefully. Remember that the vocation rehabilitation counselor is not your friend. She is being paid by the insurance carrier and her agenda is to try save the insurance company money by getting your benefits terminated—whether by finding you work, by settling your claim for little to nothing, or by terminating your benefits because you refused to cooperate with her.

4. **Do not let the vocational rehabilitation counselor into your house.** There's no reason for a rehabilitation counselor to come into your home. Always meet him or her in a public place such as a restaurant or a library. The danger of having them in your home is that it gives them access to your personal life and they will gain information about you and your family that can be turned against you. Your personal life is none of their business and you should not share your personal life with them. Here is an example. While you've not been working, you do not have your children in day care and they have been at home for obvious convenience and financial reasons. If the vocational rehabilitation counselor comes to the house and sees the children in the home, he or she may try to set you up and say that you were not cooperating because you do not want to put your children back in day care. The less the insurance company, the nurse case manager, and the vocational rehabilitation counselor know about your personal life, the better off you are.

5. **Insist on "suitable" employment.** The rules require that the job must be suitable for the employee. I've seen many times where the vocational rehabilitation counselor would instruct the worker to go to the want ads and apply for every job in the want ads. Other times, they would get a list of potential jobs from the Virginia Employment Commission and ask the employee to spend his time and money to travel around this 30 mile

radius seeking jobs without any prior determination as to whether the jobs were suitable for the worker. If you think the vocational rehabilitation specialist is violating the rules, give him or her a copy of the guidelines and ask for an explanation.

6. **Always go to job interviews**. This may seem inconsistent with the statement above about insisting on suitable employment; however, two wrongs don't make a right. Even though the vocational rehabilitation counselor may frequently violate the Virginia Workers' Compensation Commission's rules, you should keep your hands squeaky clean. Therefore, go to all interviews even though you believe that it is clear that the job is not suitable for you. There are several reasons to do this. First, you do not want to give the insurance company any reason to terminate your benefits. Even if you fail to attend a job interview that was not suitable employment for you, the insurance company may request termination of your benefits due to your lack of cooperation with their efforts. It is best not to put yourself in this position because it may mean months of waiting for a hearing without receiving a workers' compensation check. Another reason is that, if there ever is a hearing, you have done everything you are supposed to do. Therefore, you've given the defense attorney no ammunition whatsoever to be able to suggest that you should not get your workers' compensation benefits.

7. **Document, document, document**. In the appendix, I have a copy of a job search log. You can go to my website and download the form at **www. injuredworkerslawfirm.com**. As stated before, if your claim is denied, it may be many months before you ever get to a hearing and you will not be able to remember where you've looked for jobs, what activities you've done, and so forth. It is best to document everything that you do so that you will be able to refresh your memory and testify accurately. Put a **date** and **time** on all documents. Also, if the vocational rehabilitation counselor notes that you were documenting everything, she will know that you are prepared to contest any allegation that you might not be cooperating with her. Remember to document job **searching** as well as job **interviews**. If you look for a job, you need to document that just as much as if you fill out an application. This ensures all your efforts are documented. **MAKE A COPY OF EVERYTHING!**

8. **Stay in close contact with your attorney**. Usually, once a vocational rehabilitation counselor has been assigned to your case, it is the time that the insurance adjuster is most desperate in trying to cut off your benefits. The insurance company does not care if they are cut off by finding you employment or due to the appearance of a failure to cooperate on your part. You need to let your attorney know each and every time a job is offered, each time that they suggest any type of vocational training,

and anything that occurs that makes you feel uneasy. This way, the lawyer can stay on top of whether it is suitable employment and whether it's a legitimate job that you would interview for. Make sure you have your attorney advise you at each stage of this complicated process.

CHAPTER 8

Marketing, Marketing, What The Heck Is Marketing?

My answer: Lord if I only knew…The laws and exceptions are so varied, and sometimes conflicting, that it has become an easy way for insurance companies to deny benefits to deserving individuals.

If the "spirit of the law" would be followed with everyone doing the right thing, injured workers and insurance companies would both benefit. The Rule is that if an injured worker has been placed on light duty, which the employer cannot accommodate, AND the worker is NOT under an open Award Order, the injured worker needs to look for employment within his doctors' work restrictions. If you don't look for work, you don't get a weekly check. It makes a lot of common sense but how it is applied is close to pure lunacy. I have attached the marketing guidelines and a sample chart. You can also go to my website and download the forms at **www.injuredworkerslawfirm.com**.

Here Are 10 Crazy Rulings:

1. If you do not have a computer, it is not sufficient to file job applications door to door.

2. You cannot solely apply for jobs online, even when an employer requests all job applications must be filed online. Never mind that the Virginia Workers' Compensation Commission only accepts job applications online.

3. You must apply for Virginia unemployment services, even if still employed by your employer.

4. If you do not know you are supposed to look for work, along with all the detailed rules, you are still penalized and your check will be cut off.

5. If you look for work but don't write it down, you are penalized and your check will be cut off.

6. You must look for at least 5 jobs a week, even if the economy is horrible, even if you've been looking for months, even if you have no work skills, even if you think or hope you will be returning to your old job, and even if you haven't looked for a job in 25 years and really don't know where to begin.

7. You must look for at least 5 jobs a week, even if there are no jobs available in your community.

8. You must look for <u>at least</u> 5 jobs a week, even though the insurance company has denied your claim.

9. You must <u>continue</u> to look for <u>at least</u> 5 jobs a week, even when you find a job and take it, but that job is less than what you used to make hourly but has the same hours.

10. You must look for <u>at least</u> 5 jobs a week, even if you know that no employer would hire you over someone without no disabilities or injuries.

Now the ultimate problem is that all of your actions are judged AFTER the fact.

Your marketing efforts need to be "reasonable." Reasonable in your opinion? Absolutely not. Your marketing efforts need to be reasonable to the insurance company's attorney and the Deputy Commissioner that will oversee or hear your case. So, your actions will be judged by 2 people whose opinion you will not know until it is too late to change things. This creates a system where the unknowingly ignorant and injured lose benefits and the schemers can work the system to keep benefits.

So, what can you do to protect yourself? My general recommendation is somewhat overkill, but it protects you from getting benefits cut off in the first place. And, if you go to a court hearing, this could mean getting your back benefits and future benefits reinstated.

Here Are 10 Tips:

1. Document, document, document. Get specific names and phone numbers and fill out the job search chart <u>completely</u>.

2. Keep copies of evidence of job searching, along with the chart. Such as business cards, newspaper ads, and confirmation that business received your online application.

3. Look for 10 jobs a week. If you are only looking for 5 jobs and the Deputy Commissioner finds that your job search was not valid, you lose and you don't get a second chance. With 10 job searches, it will be very difficult for the insurance company's attorney to find flaws in 6 of them.

4. Follow up after you file job applications a week later and document the outcome.

5. Sign up with the Virginia Employment Commission, even if you aren't eligible for benefits.

6. Look for jobs in as many places as you can: online, in newspapers, in person, through friends, and make sure you document the source.

7. Ask your current employer for a light duty job, even if you already know they will not give you one, and document the request.

8. Turn in your job search chart weekly to your attorney. I fax them to the insurance adjuster or their attorney weekly. I do this to prove you are consistently looking for employment and that you didn't make the job searches up at a later date.

9. Don't solely look online, but some great places to look online are *careerbuilder.com, snagajob.com, craigslist.com,monster.com* and *yahoo.com.*

10. Avoid making any statements to doctors, nurses, and/ or adjuster about the stupidity of documentation. It is very sad to say, but it does not matter if you find a job, only that you look for a job per the rules.

In a recent case, my client did his entire job search by internet. He did a great job but only used one job search engine. The defense attorney cross examined the claimant and contended that he restricted his job search by only using one search engine. The claimant still won but the Deputy Commissioner said it was "troublesome" that he only used one search engine. So my new job search form is going to note that you do an internet job search, AT A MINIMUM, you need to use *Careerbuilder.com, Monster.com,* and *Snagajob.com,* as well as the Virginia Employment Commission's online resources.

CHAPTER 9

Five Tips, Four Dirty Tricks, Three Myths, Two Costly Mistakes, And Your #1 Priority

Five Tips

Tip #1 – Immediately report your injury. Report your injury to your supervisor or manager immediately, regardless of whether or not you think you will need medical treatment. Ideally, it would be best for your supervisor to write a written accident report and for you to get a copy of that report. Many jobs are physically demanding and with many jobs you have aches and pains every day. However, if you think it's a minor injury that will go away in a day or two and you don't report it and it ends up not being a minor injury, then you have given the insurance adjuster an opportunity to deny your claim and make you fight for your benefits at a hearing in order to resolve the issues. This happens often with back injuries when you may feel a little twinge when you lift a box but continue to work and by the next day you can't even get out of bed because you're in such pain. If you had reported it when it occurred, even though it was minor, they would not be able to contest it. You must report the injury within <u>30 days notice</u> of any accident, but immediately is best.

Tip #2 – Protect your rights. How do you best protect yourself? Get an Award Order by filing a claim for benefits. You may file a claim for benefits either by writing a simple letter, by filling out the claim for benefits form provided by the Virginia Workers' Compensation Commission, or by filing online at *http://www.vwc. state.va.us.* Even though I use letter form to file claim for benefits for my clients, I recommend to injured workers who do not have an attorney to use the claim for benefits form (a sample is in the appendix). You can go to my website and download the form at **www.injuredworkerslawfirm.com**. To fill the form out, you need to have the employer's name and address. The most important part of this form is "parts of your body injured." You **MUST** list **ALL** the body parts injured specifically. A shoulder is not an arm. A neck is not a shoulder. A head injury is not a brain injury. If you do not list the body part specifically, then they do not have to provide medical treatment for that body part. Overkill is best. Even if the body part doesn't need medical treatment currently, if it was injured during the accident, list it. You also need to list the specific date of injury and your average weekly wage per week. If you don't know whether the insurance adjuster is accepting or denying your claim at this point, or you believe they are accepting your claim, that's all you fill out and then you mail the form to the Virginia Workers' Compensation Commission. At that point, they will contact the insurance adjuster and require them to fill out forms that will generate the Award Order that you need. If you know they are already denying part of your claim, under Part B, you want to check the various items that are in dispute and what you are seeking: medical benefits, lost wages or partial lost wages, or permanent partial disability benefits (when a doctor has given you an impairment rating to a body part when you have lost range of motion). You can also use this form if your situation changes and you have what's called a Change in Condition, or to request a hearing on the various items that are under Part B.

Tip #3 – Keep the medical records straight. What do you need from your doctor? Two very important things: First, make sure he describes your work accident accurately in his notes. Once he is considered your workers' compensation treating physician, any opinion he has regarding your medical treatment and cause of injury is given great weight. So, make sure he has accurate information about how the accident occurred. If you feel he is rushing and doesn't understand, ask him point blank, "Do you understand what happened to me?" Doctors are human and they make mistakes in their note taking. Tell the doctor about the specific incident that happened at work. Second, always get a disability slip at each doctor's appointment, whether he has you out of work or has you on some type of work restrictions. You should never leave the doctor's office without having a disability slip. Usually, doctors will make the disability slips from one doctor appointment until the next. If your doctor's appointment gets postponed, I would suggest you call the doctor's nurse and get your work status extended. It is extremely important to make sure your attorney and your employer always have a copy of your current disability slips, and that you keep a copy for yourself. If the doctor has released you to work (such as light duty, not lifting over 10 pounds), and your supervisor asks you to lift something that's weights 20 pounds, you would have the documentation to prove that you are not allowed to do it. The important thing is to remember not to violate the work restrictions. Everybody has to abide by what the disability slip says. If the doctor says you're out of work, then you, your employer, and the insurance company are stuck with you being out of work. If it says you are released to full duty, then you, the employer, and the insurance company are stuck with you being released to full duty. If the doctor says you're released to some form of light duty, then everyone is stuck with light duty. Many employers make the injured worker feel guilty and put pressure on them to do their "fair share" and violate the doctor's work restrictions. If you violate your restrictions because your supervisor told you to lift an item heavier than your restrictions, and you are further hurt, you risk your benefits being cut off. You disobeyed your doctor's orders. Talk to a lawyer if you get into this type of situation.

Tip #4 – Get your mileage reimbursement. Currently, an injured worker can get mileage to and from medical treatment. Sometimes, injured workers may think it is too much paperwork only to get 50 ½ cents per mile reimbursed. However, there is a very easy way to do it. After you've accumulated some mileage, you simply call the medical provider's billing department and request the bill payment history. Insurance adjusters won't accept appointment cards, etc. because it does not "prove" that you were actually at the doctor's office on that day. So, the easiest way is just to get the bill payment history. Then, you go online to MapQuest. If you don't have access to the internet at home, you can go to your public library and go to MapQuest. Type in your home address, or work place if that's where you were before you went to your doctor's appointment, and type in the doctor's office address. This will give you the exact mileage. Remember to double the mileage since it is a round trip. This way, you don't have to count your miles every time or press the odometer every time you go back and forth to the doctor. If you have never requested mileage reimbursement, you can go from the date of your accident forward. You can use the sample mileage chart in the appendix. You can go to my website and download the form at **www.injuredworkerslawfirm.com**. Attach the bill payment history to the mileage chart, make a copy, and mail it to the insurance adjuster. If you have not received your mileage reimbursement within three weeks, I would recommend calling and confirming that they had received it and they are processing the request.

Tip #5 – Get your cost of living adjustment. It's a strange calculation as to when someone is eligible for COLA so many people do not request it, which can cost them a lot of money. Once, I got COLA for a client that exceeded $20,000 from previous years, plus an increase in her current weekly check by several hundred dollars. COLA is a cost of living adjustment that happens every year. In theory, if you're completely out of work and receiving workers' compensation for a while, you can request it by filling out the form, which I have included in the appendix. You can go to my website and download the form at **www.injuredworkerslawfirm.com**. You simply go to your local Social Security office, have them confirm that you are not receiving Social Security Disability benefits, mail the form to the Virginia Workers' Compensation Commission, and you can get the cost of living adjustment (you can get both if you receive Social Security Retirement benefits). If you are on Social Security Disability, you cannot get a cost of living adjustment because there is no "double dipping." Social Security gives you the cost of living adjustment. If you haven't received the cost of living adjustment for several years, you need to have a form filled out by the Social Security Administration for each year in order to get your adjustment. The trick is figuring out when you are eligible for the cost of living adjustment. You can receive your cost of living adjustment effective October 1st of each year if you are under an Open Award for temporary total disability and the accident occurred before July 1st of that same year. This means that someone who was injured on June 30 will be able to receive a cost of living adjustment as soon as October 1st (three months). Someone who was injured July 2 will not be able to receive cost of living adjustment benefits until October 1st of the *following* year (15 months).

Four Dirty Tricks

The insurance company is experienced at trying to save money and denying claims. Here are a few of the dirty tricks that I find the most appalling.

Dirty Trick #1 – Insurance adjusters voluntarily pay you some benefits. You might ask, "What's wrong with the insurance company doing what it is supposed to do?" What's wrong is that they do it in order to catch you unaware and then you are in danger of permanently losing your benefits. Many times, insurance adjusters will voluntarily make payments and will never inform the claimant of the fact that if they don't file a claim for benefits form and get an Award Order, they will quit paying them when the statute of limitations runs out, which is two years from the date of injury. This is part of their "don't ask, don't tell" policy. This occurs with entire claims and it also occurs with specific body parts. Here is an example. You have a shoulder and neck injury but the paperwork only lists your neck. The insurance company pays for your shoulder and neck medical treatment and after two years they stop your shoulder treatment. You are out of luck because every body part must be listed in the paperwork within two years of the accident for them to have to pay it. What bothers me so much about this is that most people don't want to "file a lawsuit" or "sue" their employers and they think a claim for benefits is filing a lawsuit against their employer. They don't understand that it is a requirement. The problem is that the insurance companies know this about hard working, loyal employees, and take advantage of these individuals who don't want to make waves and want to get back to work as quickly as possible. The number of times people have come to me with this problem breaks my heart, because there is nothing I can do for them at that point.

Dirty Trick #2 – Insurance adjusters record your statements. Another trick is requiring a recorded statement from you before you get paid or get medical treatment. The insurance adjusters will call you immediately, usually within two to three days of the accident, and ask to talk to you about the accident and if they can record your statement. This sounds innocent enough. However, the reason they do this is so that they can hold you to whatever you say during that initial call; even though you may still be in the hospital or on strong narcotics. You will be held responsible for what you say in that recorded statement. This is appalling to me because, while you are under extreme stress from an injury, possibly on narcotic pain medications, and just wanting to get your benefits, the insurance adjuster, as the experienced interrogator, will ask you questions and *lead* the questioning down a path that could prevent you from getting any workers' compensation benefits at all. They seem "helpful" and friendly but they are hoping to find any loophole to deny your benefits. Here is an example. One of my clients fell off a stepladder at work. While most people would think falling off a ladder at work would be covered under workers' compensation, it is not. There has to be unique circumstances surrounding falling off the ladder. Since you could fall off a ladder, fall down stairs, or trip and fall at home or someplace else just as easily, workers' compensation won't cover it. In this case, during the recorded statement, the adjuster said, "My goodness, I guess it happened so fast," and my client said, "Yes." She said, "I guess you did not know what was happening." He said, "Yes." She was basically trapping him to say he did not know how he fell off the stepladder. Through interrupting him and distracting him, she got him to say exactly what she needed for his case to be denied. Luckily, there was a portion of the statement where he did say that the ladder was a little unbalanced and had rocked beforehand. Luckily, he told his doctor when he first went to the doctor that the ladder was on uneven pavement and was rocking and he had tools in his hand and that's why he fell. Also, during recorded statements when you're telling your story, the insurance adjuster will interrupt you so that you are only answering the questions they want to hear the answer to. Their goal is not to understand your situation or to give you benefits. Their number one goal with the recorded statement is to find any loophole through which to deny benefits. This is why I usually recommend not to give recorded statements.

Dirty Trick #3 – Insurance adjusters hire private investigators. Another dirty trick of insurance adjusters is to hire private investigators to follow injured workers. They do this in contested claims and they do it in uncontested claims. They're trying to find out if the injured worker is working, is not following the doctor's work restrictions, or is capable of doing more than what has been ordered by the physician. They also have gone to neighbors' homes and asked questions. They also will follow you but only record the five seconds that **APPEAR** to be violating your work restrictions and show the recording out of context. I always advise my clients to be very cautious of who they speak to and what they do in public. It's not that they are doing anything wrong, but the appearance or suggestion that they're doing something wrong will give the insurance adjuster an opportunity to cut off benefits. While you are still unaware, they will show the tape to your doctor in order to try to have him release you to full duty work. Even if it doesn't work, it may often change the doctor's opinion of you while you have never even seen the tape or know that it exists so that you could explain it to him!

Dirty Trick #4 – Insurance adjusters want you to sign forms with wrong descriptions of injuries and wages. Whether you should sign the papers sent to you by the insurance adjuster is somewhat complicated. Yes, the agreement forms need to be signed by everyone and sent to the Commission so an award will be entered. There are two tricks the insurance adjusters play with agreement forms. First, they will have you sign the form and mail it back to them, and then they will hold onto it, never submitting it to the Virginia Workers' Compensation Commission. So you are never under an open award, which gives insured workers several advantages. The second trick is that they will not list every body part on the forms. When they don't list all the body parts and you sign off on it, you are agreeing that only your neck is hurt and not your neck and shoulder. This may seem minor but it's the crux of a lot of litigation. The second part of the form that is usually incorrect is the average weekly wage. Many times insurance adjusters will simply take the employer's word at what your average weekly wage was and put it down. This is not the accurate way to do it. The accurate way is to have them calculate your average weekly wage with a 52-week wage statement.

When this is done, all your bonuses and all your overtime is included into your average weekly wage, which gives you a higher compensation rate. Your compensation rate determines your lost wages and your permanent partial disability benefits. So it's important to have the correct amount—and obviously at the highest amount. Alleging a "mutual mistake" can sometimes fix the average weekly wage problem, but not having all the body parts listed can never be fixed after the statute of limitations has run out.

Three Myths

Myth #1 – The insurance adjuster will take care of me. They are not a good neighbor, you are not in good hands, and they are definitely not your friend. You are actually at war and at a fairly sophisticated war. The insurance adjuster is experienced and knows all the workers' compensation laws. His or her job is to save the insurance company money. Many get bonuses and recognition for saving their company money. The only way to save money is to deny claims and to pay the least amount possible. That's why they will get a nurse case manager to try to force the doctor to get you to return to work. That is why they hire private investigators to try to find any appearance that you may not be following your doctor's orders. The worst thing that they do, in my opinion, is deliberate delay. They like to delay, delay, deny, delay, delay, deny. This is their normal routine. They will delay making payments, they will delay medical treatment, they will deny that you're eligible for the MRI or some other test, then they will delay setting up your doctors' appointments, and then they will deny medical treatment by setting up a second opinion. If they do this systematically with every case, they literally save *billions* of dollars. If they delay paying out $1 million dollars for 30 days across the board with all the injured claimants that they have, they save $50,000 for one month of delays and denials *in interest alone*. One of the more egregious types of delay is denying claims frivolously while knowing that an injured worker is under a financial crunch, in order to try to get him or her to settle a claim for pennies on the dollar due to his or her financial situation. This forces the injured worker to choose between whether he should wait for approval to get medical treatment he needs or settle his claim in order just not to have his house foreclosed upon. Just remember: If there is any gray area in a case, the insurance company will deny your claim. That's why it's very important to be very clear and avoid appearances that could harm your case.

A variation of this myth is: I am a loyal employee and I will work with my employer and not file a claim because they will treat me right. Perhaps you are afraid to file claim thinking you will lose your job. Maybe you don't want to feel like you are being greedy or "one of those people who sue."

In reality, when you fail to file a claim and assert your rights, you are actually losing your rights. It is very black and white. You file a claim and future benefits are protected. You don't file a claim, benefits are lost. The most common situation is that you think you will get better and want to continue to work through the pain. Coworkers and your supervisor help you with parts of your job you can't do. Your supervisor says you can make a claim later if you have to. Your coworkers remind you of the steak dinner party when the team goes 100 days without an accident or injury. A few months go by and the pain continues to increase and finally you tell your supervisor that you know something is seriously wrong. He says it is too late and if you can't do your job, he will have to let you go. He may even say he doesn't recall any injury.

The consequences are that you are fired because you really can't do it anymore; you lose your health insurance and can't afford to pay out-of-pocket for any medical care. When you finally file a claim, the insurance company denies it stating either no accident or failure to make a timely report or failure to give notice within 30 days.

Myth #2 – The insurance adjuster or my employer says I don't have a claim, so I guess I don't. As said before, insurance adjusters deny valid claims all of the time and most of the time they do this to save their insurance company money. Many injured persons won't pursue, and they save money. Think about all the cases they deny. In my opinion, 75% are definite to possible valid claims. If half of the workers accept the explanation for the denial, then the insurance company walks away not having to pay 35% of the valid claims, again taking millions of dollars unjustifiably away from injured workers. At the very least, denial creates a four to six month delay, which saves the insurance company a lot of money. Many employers try to trick an injured worker by saying that if you didn't notify us within 24 hours of the accident we're not going to accept your case. It may be true that they will litigate the matter but that does not mean that you are not entitled to file a claim and get benefits. You actually have two years to file a claim. You have to notify your employer within 30 days of your injury. It really is not the employer's decision or the insurance adjuster's decision to make. It is the Virginia Workers' Compensation Commission that makes the decision whether you are entitled to workers' compensation benefits. Once, I actually had a client who was injured at work and his employer asked him not to file a workers' compensation claim so the employer's workers' compensation insurance rates would not go up. The employee agreed and signed a note in front of witnesses saying he was giving up all his workers' compensation rights. Obviously, when all his vacation and sick leave was gone and he was looking at two more major surgeries, he did not know what to do. Luckily, he came to me and we prevailed at his hearing because he had given notice within 30 days and we filed within the two-year statute of limitations. It was of no consequence that he had signed something to that effect.

Myth #3 – A workers' compensation claim is just like a personal injury claim. Unfortunately, on most levels, workers' compensation is definitely not like other personal injury claims. It is the injured workers' only remedy in the sense that they can't sue their employer for injuries that occurred on the job. Also, in a personal injury case, you're supposed to be made "whole" and you get compensated for pain and suffering and aggravation. However, in a workers' compensation claim, you get two thirds of your wages weekly, and your medical bills paid and you never get anything for the aggravation, the financial stress, etc. of what occurred from the accident. Also, everything has to be approved by the Virginia Workers' Compensation Commission, including attorney fees and settlements. The insurance company and the injured worker can't make a "private" agreement.

Two Costly Mistakes

Mistake #1 – Hiding old injuries and accidents or misrepresenting your actual activity level. Under workers' compensation, aggravations of pre-existing conditions are covered but many people believe that if they had a prior back injury or prior auto accident, it will harm their workers' compensation case. They believe no one will ever know or find out about the past so they don't inform their lawyer, or when they are asked in a recorded statement by the insurance adjuster, they deny past injuries. Under workers' compensation, there is no doctor/patient privilege so the insurance adjuster can have access to all your medical records (past and present) and will clearly find out about old injuries and accidents. Also, they have access to databases and will do criminal background checks, look on their own databases to see if you filed any previous workers' compensation claims, etcetera. It's always much better to deal with the issue up front, in the beginning, than trying to explain why the matter was hidden.

Misrepresenting your actual activity level is also very costly. This can go both ways. There are many "fake" diagnostic tests that are given to injured workers by the workers' compensation doctors and physical therapists. One test is called the Waddell test. These tests try to determine if you are faking your injury. Obviously, always give your best effort. The opposite end of the spectrum is stating that you can do things that you actually can't do. Hoping and wishing is not the same as doing a physical activity consistently, every day, every week, for years. Many people who are eager to get back to work want their doctors to return them back to work full duty since they are paid more when working than when they're under workers' compensation and their families are suffering. However, this can cause more serious injuries to the person. It is important to represent your abilities accurately to your doctors and medical providers. I recently had a client posting on Facebook: "going to Hawaii to go surfing," "can't wait until I receive my million dollar settlement," and "headed to Colorado to go snowboarding." Obviously, he was not doing any of these things and when asked at his hearing why he posted those things he stated it was to "pick up chicks." Well, he lost his case because he was either lying online or lying at his hearing and his credibility was shot. So, another tip is to clean up your Twitter, Facebook, or Google+ accounts and any other social networks that you belong to and tighten your privacy settings so you know who can see your posts before you post anything that could be used against you. Insurance adjusters and private investigators look at these sites regularly. I tell people when I meet with them to please tell me everything, even the things they perceive as bad or hurtful to their case. I can deal and work around "bad" facts, but I can NEVER fix it when my client has been labeled a "liar," innocently or not.

Mistake #2 – Failing to report your claim and to file your claim. As stated several times earlier, even if it's a minor claim you need to report it, simply because most serious injuries related to the neck, back, shoulders and knees seem minor and then they turn out to be more severe. With these types of permanent nerve damage, you may never return to your former physical abilities. Clearly, if you're in a serious auto accident you're not going to have an issue, but it's the more subtle injuries that can be the most overlooked. The second part is failure to file a claim. Again, just because they're making voluntary payments does not mean that they will continue to do so. They will only do so for two years unless you file the claim for benefits. I've had many people come to me after the two year statute of limitations has run out and they have been devastated to find out that they thought the insurance adjusters were helping them when, in fact, they were just biding their time to be able to cut off benefits. It's much cheaper for them to pay lost wages for two years than it is for them to pay lost wages for nine and a half years and medical benefits for life.

Your First Priority—Getting The Highest Recovery

Your number one priority is to get the maximum/highest recovery possible. Under workers' compensation, you are never made "whole," so you need to make sure you get the most that you can to head off any financial or health disasters. There are two parts of getting the highest recovery: medical and financial. Of the two, the most important is your health. The obvious goal is to get your health back to where it was prior to the accident. The best steps to take to protect your health: 1) You want to get treatment as soon as possible; 2) If you continue having medical problems, continue to complain to the workers' compensation doctor, and insist on treatment; 3) If you think your workers' compensation physician is not taking your interests to heart, you are entitled to a second opinion; 4) There are ways, though they are very hard, to change your treating physician; and 5) Discuss with your attorney how to get the best medical treatment possible in your particular case.

The second part of getting the highest recovery is financial. First, you need to see if you have any other types of non-workers' compensation benefits or claims you may have in addition to your workers' compensation claim. If you are in an auto accident at work and a non-coworker was at fault, this is an auto personal injury claim. The equipment you were using was defective. This is a products liability claim. If you were in a parking lot owned by someone that's not your employer, you may have a premise liability claim. Other non-workers' compensation benefits are Social Security, short term disability, long term disability, veterans' benefits, regular health insurance, retirement benefits with your employer, or possibly unemployment benefits. It's important to coordinate all of these aspects with your workers' compensation claim to make sure you get the most money available. A work injury is financially devastating. Your paycheck is automatically cut by one third but your bills and financial obligations are not cut by one third. Additionally, if your claim is denied, you may be looking at six months before you have a hearing and a decision is rendered and you begin to receive a weekly check. All this puts injured workers behind in their bills, their mortgages, and their car payments. So, if there's any way to make you "whole" it would be ideal to search out all avenues and not just workers' compensation. Second, maximize the workers' compensation financial benefits. Obviously, to maximize the financial aspect of your workers' compensation claim, follow the tips in this book so that there is no "gray" area in your case so the workers' compensation insurance adjuster has to send your financial weekly payments to you. Third, coordinate the settlement of your workers' compensation benefits with the other types of benefits you may have. There may come a time in your case where it will be best for you to settle your workers' compensation claim while coordinating it with the other types of benefits you have. This is a complicated process of weighing the pros and cons. The consequences can be devastating if the settlement is not done properly. An individual who had lost his left leg at the knee came into my office, once. He was very proud that he had settled his workers' compensation claim for $75,000 without an attorney. However, he didn't understand why, when he was awarded Social Security disability benefits, he wasn't getting the correct monthly check from Social Security. Social Security disability is offset by any workers' compensation benefits received. Unfortunately, language that should have been in his workers' compensation settlement documents protecting his Social Security benefits and his Medicare benefits were not in there. He actually settled, in effect, for nothing because his $75,000 was counted as his Social Security monthly check and he would not get the full amount from Social Security for over five years. There are similar complications with settling personal injury claims while on workers' compensation. Workers' compensation has a lien on any personal injury claim. It is best to seek out legal advice when attempting to settle your claims to maximize the most you can get. There is no doubt in my mind that if an injured person hires an experienced workers' compensation attorney, he or she will get the maximum recovery.

CHAPTER 10

Frequently Asked Questions

What Are My Rights And Benefits?

Here are a few common questions that I get. If you want additional information, go to my website at **www.injuredworkerslawfirm.com.** Also, if you have a specific question that is not answered, go to my website and submit your question. I will answer it as best as I can.

Q: I got hurt at work, but it was my fault, so I don't have a case. Right?

A: Wrong. Workers' compensation is a no-fault system. It doesn't matter if the accident occurred because you made a mistake or a coworker made a mistake or no one is to blame.

Q: I was out of work for two weeks but they only paid me for one week. Can the insurance company do that?

A: Yes. You do not get paid for lost wages for the first seven days you are out of work unless you are out of work for twenty-one days or more. So, if you are out of work less than a week you will receive no workers' compensation lost wage benefits. If you are out of work two weeks, you get one week of workers' compensation pay. If you are out of work three weeks, you get three weeks of workers' compensation pay.

Q: What benefits am I entitled to if workers' compensation accepts my work injury as compensable?

A: If your injury is deemed compensable by your employer's workers' compensation insurance carrier, you are entitled to payment of your lost wages (two thirds of your average weekly wage) up to 500 weeks, payment for a permanent partial impairment rating if the physicians feels you have a permanent loss of use of a body part because of your work injury if your wage loss is less than 500 weeks, medical expenses that are reasonable and necessary authorized by your workers' compensation treating physician, and reimbursement for your out-of-pocket expenses including prescriptions and mileage traveled.

Q: Are my workers' compensation benefits taxable?
A: No.

Q: Does the permanent partial disability rating I was given by my workers' compensation treating physician take into account my pain and suffering?

A: No. There is no compensation for pain and suffering. Your permanent partial disability rating is only based upon loss of range of motion.

Q: I have just been given a permanent partial disability rating and am still receiving my lost wage check. Can I get both?

A: No. You cannot get both temporary total disability benefits at the same time you receive permanent partial disability benefits. However, once you return to work, even if at a lower wage, you can get temporary partial disability benefits and permanent partial disability benefits at the same time, but each week will count as two weeks.

Q: How often will I receive my total temporary disability check and what do I do if I don't receive it on time?

A: You should receive your total temporary disability check on a weekly or bi-weekly basis. If you don't receive it on time, contact the insurance adjuster to request an explanation. If you're under an Award and your check is more than two weeks late, you can also request to receive additional money from the insurance company (a 20 percent late payment penalty).

Q: My son died in a work accident and has no dependents. What happens?

A: If a deceased worker has no dependents, then only related medical expenses and up to $10,000 for burial expenses will be paid.

Q: I settled my workers' compensation claim without a lawyer. Can I re-open the claim?

A: No. Once the appeal time has passed from the settlement order, you cannot re-open your settled claim.

Q: I'm afraid I'll be fired if I file a workers' compensation claim. Can my employer do this?

A: No. Virginia law does not allow an employer to fire an employee in retaliation for filing a workers' compensation claim. If you believe that your employer fired you in retaliation for filing a claim, contact the Virginia Department of Labor to file a complaint.

Q: I think someone is following me. Would a workers' compensation insurance adjuster hire a private detective to follow me?

A: Yes. When your injury is serious enough that it requires you to be out of work for an extended period of time, you almost certainly will be under surveillance by a private detective who will probably follow you around taking video footage of your activities. Because of the strong likelihood of being followed, you should assume that you are being followed and act accordingly.

Q: The insurance adjuster has offered that I settle my case but I don't have a lawyer. What should I do?

A: It will be very difficult for you to know what your case is worth and whether the insurance company has offered you a fair settlement offer. You should definitely hire a lawyer to assist you in the settlement so that you can get the maximum recovery. If your case is very minor and does not involve you being out of work for any substantial period of time or any permanent injuries, you do not necessarily need a lawyer. However, you should still probably get a consultation from a lawyer before settling a case, even if it's a relatively small case.

Q: How long do I receive workers' compensation benefits?

A: You can receive your lost wages and permanent partial disability benefits for a maximum of 500 weeks between the two benefits. Your medical benefits are lifetime as long as the doctor says the medical treatment is caused by the original work injury, and it's reasonable and necessary medical treatment, and you go to the authorized treating physician.

Q: I got fired so I no longer get benefits. Right?

A: Wrong. You continue with your medical benefits.
Most likely, you will continue to receive your weekly check (or it would start up again). The only reasons your weekly check would stop would be if the doctor had released you to full duty or you were fired for willful misconduct.

Q: I was put on FMLA leave without applying for it. Can my employer do this?

A: If you have an injury that qualified under the FMLA statute, the employer is required by law to implement FMLA whether you ask for it or not; whether you want it or not. It is perfectly legal to use FMLA for a workers' compensation injury; the two are not mutually exclusive. It's not one or the other.

Returning To Work

Q: What if my employer offers me a job within my doctor's light duty work restrictions, but I do not want to take the job?

A: If you choose not to accept the light duty position that you are offered, then you are not entitled to lost wages.

Q: The workers' compensation treating physician has said I can return back to my job on light duty but my employer says there is no light duty, and I cannot come back until I have no restrictions. What happens?

A: You will continue to receive your lost wage check (total temporary disability benefits) until you are released to full duty or your restrictions become permanent and the insurance company finds you a job within your restrictions. If you are not under an Award, though, I would recommend that you look for work until you can get under an Award.

Q: Can I take a new job with a different employer while I'm receiving workers' compensation benefits?

A: Yes, but your eligibility for lost benefits may be affected.

Q: I cannot return to my job because of my work injury and this is the only type of job I've ever had. Am I permanently and totally disabled?

A: No, not necessarily. By law, to be permanently and totally disabled you have to have a significant loss of use of two extremities, eyes, ears, or a have had a traumatic brain injury that has left you unable to use those body parts in gainful employment in order to be able to seek permanent total disability benefits.

Am I Covered By Workers' Compensation?

Q: I have an old injury that began bothering me when I injured myself at work. Will this injury be covered even though it is pre-existing?

A: Yes, aggravations of preexisting conditions are covered under workers' compensation. As long as your physician says that the accident at work aggravated your preexisting condition, then you will get workers' compensation benefits.

Q: My daughter is a minor and she was injured on the job. Is she covered?

A: A minor is covered by the Act. If the minor meets the requirement of being an employee, she is entitled to workers' compensation benefits.

Q: I'm employed by a staffing agency. Can I get workers' compensation benefits if I'm injured at work?

A: Yes, the staffing agency would be liable for your workers' comp benefits if you were injured at one of your places of employment.

Q: What if my employer says he doesn't have workers' compensation insurance, and I get hurt at work?

A: You can contact the Virginia Workers' Compensation Commission to confirm whether your employer has workers' compensation insurance. If the employer does not have workers' compensation insurance, the Virginia Workers' Compensation Commission will take action against your employer. He will be assessed penalties. Additionally, there is the Uninsured Employer's Fund, which would pay your benefits and then seek reimbursement from your employer.

Q: Are psychological injuries covered by the Act?

A: Possibly. Psychological injuries alone such as stress, depression, or anxiety are not covered under the Act unless there was a sudden shock or fright. However, if your work injury and/or the chronic pain from the injury causes you stress, anxiety, and depression, then it will be covered. There has to be a physical or bodily change in the body, or a sudden shock or fright that caused the psychological injury for the psychological injury to be covered.

Q: I am a truck driver who lives in another state but was injured in Virginia. In which state should I file a workers' compensation claim?

A: Generally, you should file a claim for workers' compensation in Virginia if you were injured in Virginia.

Q: Is it necessary for me to be a United States citizen to collect workers' compensation benefits?

A: No. You do not have to a citizen nor do you have to be properly documented in order to collect workers' compensation benefits. However, you may not receive some wage loss benefits if you are not legally able to work in the U. S.

Q: How long do I have to be employed before I'm entitled to workers' compensation benefits?

A: There is no required length of time. If you are injured at work in the first hour of the first day of employment you will be entitled to full workers' compensation benefits.

Q: Can I get workers' comp if I'm injured as a result of horseplay on the part of my coworker?

A: Possibly. The law is changing so double check with an attorney. If both you and a co-worker are engaged in horseplay or a fight, it has been considered personal and not related to employment.

Q: If I'm injured while traveling to work, can I get workers' compensation benefits?

A: The answer in most cases is no. Workers' compensation does not protect workers who are injured while traveling to or from work. There are certain exceptions, however. For instance, a traveling salesman who has to drive regularly in his work can recover even if he is traveling to the first sales appointment of the day.

Q: I was under the influence of alcohol when my on-the-job accident happened. Can I still recover?

A: Most likely, no. There can be no recovery if the worker is intoxicated or under the influence of controlled substances and if that intoxication caused the injuries. If you misstepped or used poor judgment with machinery, intoxication would be the cause and you would not get benefits. However, if you are under the influence of alcohol and are a passenger in a vehicle and another vehicle hits you, you could get workers' compensation benefits. It would be compensable because being under the influence was not the cause of the accident.

Medical Concerns

Q: If my doctor recommends certain treatments, tests, or surgery since I have lifetime medical benefits, will the workers' compensation carrier always have to pay for it?

A: No. Often when medical care starts to get expensive or take a long time, insurance adjusters begin denying treatment. They have the nurse case manager try to change the doctor's opinion. They will hire another doctor to say the treatment is not necessary or related to the accident. They will use gaps in treatment to allege current symptoms are not related. After months of waiting for a hearing, you may get the surgery approved by the Commission, but there is just as much of a chance that the Commission believes their doctor—and you don't get the treatment you need. Also, remember the injured worker has the burden of proof. If it is a tie, you lose.

Q: I received a doctor's bill even though it was for a doctor visit authorized by the insurance adjuster. What do I do?

A: You are not responsible for any of the medicals bills that are incurred as long as you are being treated by the authorized workers' compensation treating physician. The best step to take is to mail a copy of it to the insurance adjuster and also call the billing department of the medical provider and tell them to mail the bill directly to the insurance adjuster. Give them the workers' compensation insurance claim number and adjuster's name and phone number.

Q: I don't like the workers' compensation doctor. Can I choose a different doctor?

A: No. If you choose a different doctor or choose to stop seeing the workers' compensation treating physician, then your benefits may be terminated or suspended for unjustifiable refusal of medical treatment. In Virginia, once an authorized treating physician has been established, that is the only doctor the insurance carrier has to pay. If you seek treatment with a non-authorized treating physician, you will be responsible for paying for that treatment. There are ways to get a new treating physician but it is difficult and best to discuss strategy with your attorney.

Q: While receiving physical therapy for my work related back injury, the physical therapist did something to my shoulder and now my shoulder hurts constantly. It never hurt before physical therapy. Who's responsible for my new shoulder injury?

A: Any new injuries which are caused by the medical treatment offered by your employer remain the responsibility of your employer. It will be covered by workers' compensation.

Q: I feel uncomfortable when my nurse case manager insists on coming into the examination room while I'm being seen by the doctor. Is there anything I can do.

A: You have the right to request that she wait outside of the room during the examination. After the exam, she may discuss the exam with the doctor. If the case manager still insists on coming into the room, ask your doctor to have her leave.

Q: What doctor will treat me for my work-related injuries?

A: If the insurance company accepts responsibility for your accident and pays your claim, the insurance company gets to dictate your medical care to a certain degree. The insurance company is allowed to give you a panel of 3 physicians from which you pick one. Once a treating doctor is established, neither you nor the employer can "doctor shop" by sending you to doctor after doctor until getting the desired result. If the insurance adjuster denies the claim, you may pick which doctor you want and when you prevail at your hearing, the insurance company is stuck with that doctor.

Q: What happens if my condition gets worse after my benefits have stopped, and I need to go back out of work?

A: If your condition worsens and a doctor takes you back out of work, you can apply for additional benefits. This is called a change in condition application. You must do so, however, within two years from the date the last compensation payment was made pursuant to an Award order. If you've been voluntarily paid sporadically, this does not stop the two years from running. This is another reason why its' very important always to get your Award Orders entered for all benefits and time periods.

Q: Can I tell my workers' compensation treating physician confidential information?

A: No. Under workers' compensation there is no physician/patient privilege. Your doctor can tell your employer and the insurance carrier anything she learns from you regarding your workers' compensation case and your injury or illness.

Q: Is my case over when the doctor sends me back to work?

A: No. If you are getting the same pay as before, then you could start getting your weekly permanent partial disability check. Your medical benefits continue. Also, if circumstances change, your temporary total disability benefits may get reinstated.

Q: I recently settled my workers' compensation claim and I still need medical treatment. Medicare has told me they will not cover my work injury until I have accumulated enough medical bills from treating on my own to equal the amount of the workers' compensation Award. Is this correct?

A: Yes. If all or a portion of your settlement was meant to cover the cost of future medical treatment for your injury, Medicare is entitled to do this. In situations where the settlement includes payment for future medical care, it's very important that a portion of the settlement is allocated towards Medicare so that they will not do this. If you are in this type of situation, it is best to have an attorney help you settle your workers' compensation claim. Unfortunately, in your case you cannot "redo" your workers' compensation settlement to protect the money from Medicare.

CHAPTER 11

So You're Asking Yourself, Do I Need An Attorney?

Hiring a lawyer can cause some stress because for most of us it's a very unfamiliar process. People want to make sure the lawyer understands the issues and will work hard to represent their interests. You must weigh the benefits versus the cost of hiring a lawyer. There are obviously numerous benefits. There's peace of mind in having someone who knows exactly what to do for you and how to guide you in the right direction to get the maximum benefits available. The cost of an attorney varies with each case. Most attorneys who represent injured workers are paid with what is called a "contingency fee," which means the lawyer's fee depends on his success in resolving the case. The fee comes out of whatever you are awarded for your claims. Usually, the lawyer takes 20 percent of the gross settlement. This arrangement works well for most parties because the lawyer takes a risk that he'll never get paid if the claim goes nowhere, and the client gets to pursue his claim without having to come up with thousands of dollars up front in legal fees and costs. Without this arrangement, some people would never be able to fight a claim because they would not be able to afford it. If a case is not settled, you may be charged a contingency fee of 15 percent if an attorney helps you get your permanent partial disability benefits. You may be charged a fee of a few hundred dollars for each contested hearing your attorney attends. That fee, though, is usually paid through the recovery of future awards that you receive through your workers' compensation claim. For example, if an attorney is awarded a $300 attorney fee, it would be paid from your awarded weekly check at $25 per week. We all want to keep our expenses down but sometimes you have to pay for expertise and the same holds true for a workers' compensation attorney. When you're talking about trying to replace a portion of your income you've lost from being hurt on the job and your health, you really can't afford to handle the case yourself and risk making a crucial mistake. Thus, in the majority of cases you would need an attorney. However, there are some situations where you may not need an attorney. For example, if you have not missed any time from work and you've only had one doctor's appointment which cost $100; even if it's contested, it would be unwise to pay an attorney $300 to recover a $100 doctor's visit bill. If it is contested and you have health insurance, submit it under your regular insurance and you only have to pay a co-pay. On the opposite end of the spectrum, for someone who will never be able to return to work and will need extensive medical treatment, the risk is too high not to have an experienced attorney working for you. A 1999 study found that insurance companies pay higher settlements to injured people who use an attorney than those who do not. It's true. The insurance industry performed a study and found that people who had accident claims received more money in settlement by using an attorney than those who settled on their own. The study was performed by the Insurance Research Council, a non-profit organization that's supported by leading property and casualty insurance companies across the United States. The Insurance Research Council found that people who use an attorney received on average 3½ times more money in settlement than those individuals who settled on their own. Since most workers' compensation attorneys offer free consultations, you can discuss the need for an attorney at the meeting.

So, how do I find an experienced workers' compensation attorney in my area? Here are some tips.

1. **Get a referral from an attorney that you know.** He or she will probably know someone who specializes in your area of need. If you need an attorney in an area of practice that we don't handle, call us and we'll help you find the right lawyer for your case.

2. **Get a recommendation from someone who has actually used that lawyer for the same type of case you have.** Hiring your deadbeat brother-in-law's DUI attorney for your workers compensation case might not be a good idea.

3. **Visit internet rating sites.** They are pretty good. Avvo.com, Superlawyers.com, Lawyers.com and Nolo. com are reputable. You might also check the BBB.org (Better Business Bureau), to see if the law firm is rated and in good standings.

4. **Check to see whether your lawyer is a specialist.** Virginia has no state specific specialization process, but many experienced attorneys are members of specific organizations regarding specific areas of the law.

5. **To get a good "feel" for a lawyer,** call the office and ask for any books or articles they have written and CD's or DVD's on your case subject area that they have recorded. Most lawyers will gladly send you their new client information package.

Again, this isn't, by any means, a complete list. You need to do your homework. Visit websites, watch YouTube videos, and make in-person appointments.

What Does An Experienced Workers' Compensation Attorney Do For You?

Here is a more or less complete list of the tasks your attorney may be called upon to do in your case. Remember, each case is different and not all these tasks are required in every case.

1. Conduct the initial interview with the client.

2. Educate the client about workers' compensation claims and the specific issues in his or her claim.

3. Gather the evidence: medical records, payroll information, personnel files, etc.

4. Analyze the issues to see if there are any third party claims that may be available for the claimant.

5. Analyze the legal issues, such as willful misconduct and medical causation.

6. Talk to the claimant's physicians or obtain written reports from them to fully understand the client's medical condition.

7. Analyze the validity of any liens on the case that may be asserted.

8. Contact the workers' compensation insurance company and the Virginia Workers' Compensation Commission, put them on notice of the claim and file the claim for benefits, if this has not already been done.

9. Decide with the client whether an attempt will be made to negotiate the case with the insurance company to settle the case.

10. If there has been a request for a hearing, prepare the client, witnesses, and medical providers for depositions.

11. Prepare written questions and answers and take the depositions of physicians, the claimant, and other witnesses.

12. Prepare the client and witnesses for the hearing.

13. Organize and prepare the medical exhibits.

14. Take the case to the hearing and make recommendations to the client as to whether or not to appeal the case.

15. Advise the client throughout the case on various issues such as issues with nurse case managers, vocational rehabilitation specialists, employers, and insurance adjusters.

16. Assist in getting mileage paid, prescriptions filled, and cost of living adjustments.

Our Services

If you or someone you know has been injured or has any questions regarding the content of this book please feel free to contact us at 1-877-755-7744 or 1-804-755-7755. It is always advisable to seek counsel early on in a workers' compensation case for the simple fact that it's easier to head off a potential problem than to fix one that's already occurred.

Injured Workers Law Firm

At my firm, we pride ourselves on personal service. If your case meets our criteria for acceptance, you can be assured that you will receive close personal attention. We will keep you advised as to all aspects of the stages of your case and keep you fully informed of all developments. You can call on us at any time with questions about your case. When your case is ready to be resolved, we will carefully advise you as to whether your case should be settled or whether you should continue receiving your workers' compensation benefits. If we do have a hearing in your case, we will consult with you at every stage of the case and decide together what witnesses would be best to be called at the hearing. Our initial consultation with you is absolutely free. After the consultation, there is absolutely no obligation to hire us. If we decide together that we will represent you in your case, we will do so on a contingency basis unless specified otherwise. If you have any questions about your case, please call and we will be happy to speak with you and help you any way we can.

I hope this book serves as a helpful reference tool for you to understanding workers' compensation. Just having a grasp of some of the terminology you will encounter will make you feel more comfortable with the process and will allow you to speak in a more knowledgeable way with your attorney. The issues involved in a workers' compensation claim are, in fact, highly technical and complicated. You can make a go of it on your own but hiring an attorney who has expertise in this specialty will likely ease your stress and net you more money by the end of the process. Remember to select an attorney who focuses on and handles a lot of workers' compensation cases. Just having a law degree doesn't make the lawyer competent in this technical field. If you think we can help you with your case, please feel free to call us. We will be glad to talk to you and see if we are the right attorneys for you and your case.

FREE NEWSLETTERS

From Injured Workers Law Firm

Would you like some practical advice on how to deal with insurance companies? Would you like to learn about interesting developments in the law that can affect your life? At Injured Workers Law Firm, we produce a newsletter that provides you with this type of information and other various aspects of the law. We cover topics such as the types of insurance that you should have with regards to your home and automobiles. We also include articles regarding hot topics in various areas of the law. We strongly believe that arming our clients with knowledge about the legal system and varied aspects of the law can help avoid many legal disputes. We also encourage our clients to contact us if there is a particular subject that they would like for us to cover in our newsletters. We will always strive to keep our newsletter both informative and entertaining. If you'd like to receive our newsletter, free of charge, you can either fax the following form to (804) 612-1724 or mail the form to Injured Workers Law

Firm, 7826 Shrader Road, Richmond, Virginia 23294. You may also go to our website at *injuredworkerslawfirm.com* and request to be added to our newsletter subscription list.

Please start my subscription for your free newsletters.

Name:_____

Address:_____

City:_____

Zip Code: _____

Fax or mail this form to Injured Workers Law Firm at:

7826 Shrader Road
Richmond, Virginia 23294
804-755-7755 or 877-755-7744 toll free
804-612-1724 fax

Michele S. Lewane

Michele Lewane has been representing injured workers against insurance companies since 1990. She limits her practice to workers' compensation.

Michele is the lead attorney in workers' compensation matters at Injured Workers' Law Firm. After completing her undergraduate degree at the University of Virginia, she graduated in the top of her class from the University of Richmond, T.C. Williams School of Law in 1989. Immediately following law school, she clerked for the State Court of Appeals, gaining extensive experience and insight into workers' compensation matters by researching and drafting opinions on the technical aspects of this area of law. In 1990, Michele began practicing as an attorney, partnering with Hubard, Samuels, and Lewane. By 2002, Michele Lewane had significantly narrowed the areas of law she practiced. She was emphasizing Domestic and Workers' Compensation. By 2004, MSL, P.C. had positioned itself solely as a workers' compensation law firm. By 2008, MSL, P.C.

changed its location and name to Injured Workers' Law Firm. In 2007, she created Injured Workers' Law Firm to help injured workers exclusively with their workers' compensation needs. Be sure to visit *injuredworkerslawfirm. com* for a lot of useful information. Michele has lectured and written about various areas of the law, including workers' compensation seminars for other lawyers. She is a member of many professional organizations, including the Virginia Trial Lawyers' Association and Workers' Injury Law and Advocacy Group. Michele is a native of Richmond, with deep connections in this community. Her passion to help injured workers initiated the formation of the Virginia Chapter of Kid's Chance, an organization offering scholarships to children of injured workers.

Appendix

Form and Instructions to Get Cost of Living Increases

VIRGINIA R. DIAMOND,
Chairman

WILLIAM L. DUDLEY, JR.,
Commissioner

JAMES J. SZABLEWICZ, Chief
Deputy Commissioner

COMMONWEALTH of VIRGINIA

Workers' Compensation Commission
1000 DMV Drive
Richmond, Virginia 23220
www.vwc.state.va.us

IRIS C. PEACE, Clerk

Claims Examination
Department
1-877-664-2566

US Social Security Administration - Benefits

vs.

Accident Date: _____

VWC File No.: _____

Please provide the requested information in order that we may determine entitlement to cost of living adjustment for a workers' compensation claim.

Name: _____

Address: _____

Social Security #: _____

(Please print SSN legibly in the blank)

Is the above named individual receiving Social Security Disability benefits?

❏ Yes (Please answer question 2)

❏ No (Thank you for your assistance)

Please indicate the monthly amount of Social Security Disability benefits including the Medicare deductible and the dates benefits were paid:

$ _____ Gross monthly Social Security benefit amount

$ _____ Monthly Medicare premium deduction

$ _____ Net monthly Social Security benefit amount

Dates: _____

Requested by: _____

Claimant's signature Date

Prepared by:_____
Social Security RepresentativeDate

Telephone # ( ) -

COLA/Social Security Verification Request
VWC Form No. CA51 (rev. 09/28/07)

Filing Instructions
COLA/Social Security Verification Request
VWC Form No. CA51

In order to apply for a Cost-of-Living Adjustment, please complete the following steps:

1. Complete the upper portion of the eligibility form to include the claimant's name, accident date, VWC File Number, and Social Security Number.

2. Take the form to the US Social Security Administration. A representative of the US Social Security Administration must complete Sections 1 and 2.

3. The eligibility form must be signed by a US Social Security Representative.

4. The eligibility form must be signed by the Claimant.

5. Return the form to the Virginia Workers' Compensation Commission for Cost-of-Living eligibility determination.

Please Note:

In the event that Social Security Benefits are not being received, the signature of the US Social Security Representative is still required.

For questions or assistance with completing the form, please contact the Claims Examination Department using the Commission's Toll-free number at 1-877-664-2566 or visit the website at *www.vwc.state.va.us*.

Mileage Reimbursement Form

Claimant's Name: _____

Address: _____

Employer: _____

Date of Accident: _____

Date of Birth: _____

Social Security Number: _____

Date	Traveled From (include address)	Traveled To (Include name and address of doctor, hospital, therapist, etc.)	Round Trip Mileage	Parking (Include receipts)	Bridge Tolls (Include receipts)	Public Trans/Other (Include receipts)
	Total Miles		x $.555 =		$	
	Total Parking		$	$	$	
	Total Bridge Tolls			$	$	
	Total Public Transportation/Other				$	
	REIMBURSEMENT				$	

Table of Weeks for Loss of Use of a Body Part

Loss	Compensation Period
1. Thumb	60 weeks
2. First finger (index finger)	35 weeks
3. Second finger	30 weeks
4. Third finger	20 weeks
5. Fourth finger (little finger)	15 weeks
6. First phalanx of the thumb or any other finger	one-half compensation
7. Great toe	30 weeks
8. A toe other than a great toe	10 weeks
9. First phalanx of any toe	one-half compensation
10. Hand	150 weeks
11. Arm	200 weeks
12. Foot	125 weeks
13. Leg	175 weeks
14. Permanent total loss of the vision of an eye	100 weeks
15. Permanent total loss of hearing of an ear	50 weeks
16. Severely marked disfigurement of the body resulting from an injury not otherwise compensated by this section	not exceeding 60 weeks

Claim Form & Request for Hearing and Instructions

Virginia Workers' Compensation Commission
1000 DMV Drive Richmond Virginia 23220
1-877-664-2566
www.vwc.state.va.us

_____

Jurisdiction Claim #

_____

Claim Administrator #

SEE FOLLOWING PAGES FOR INSTRUCTIONS

Injured Workers Name: _____

Address: _____

City: _____ State: _____ Zip: _____

Home Phone: _____

Work Phone: _____

Employers Name: _____

Address: _____

City: _____ State: _____ Zip: _____

Employers Phone: _____

Parts of Body Injured: _____

Date of Injury*: _____ Average Earnings per week: _____

* in case of disease, give date doctor told you that disease was caused by work

PART A (Claim Form) (All injured workers should complete this section for workers' compensation injuries)

I hereby file this claim to protect my rights under the Virginia Workers' Compensation Act for the injury or disease described above. I am not requesting the Commission take any specific action at this time.

_____

Injured Worker's signature

_____

Print Name

_____

Date

Please sign and return to the Commission. Complete Part B below **only** if you are requesting a hearing.

Part B (Request for Hearing) (You are not required to complete this section—do so only if you are requesting a hearing)

I hereby request a hearing from the Commission. I am seeking the following:

_____ An Award for medical benefits for my injury (including any treatment already received & paid for) **

_____ I missed work because of my injury on (dates) _____ **

_____ I earned less pay because of my injury on (dates) _____ **

_____ I have a loss of or loss of use of a body part or have disfigurement. **

_____ I have unpaid medical bills relating to my injury. **
Other _____

_____

_____
Injured Worker's signature

_____
Print Name

_____

Date

** Attach medical records or bills.

If there are any questions regarding this form, please contact the Commission toll-free at **1-877-664-2566**.

Claim Form & Request for Hearing

Filing Instructions

1. Even if you have been paid by your employer or claim administrator for time missed from work because of your injury or for medical treatment for your injury, you must file a claim with the Virginia Workers' Compensation Commission to protect your right to benefits under Virginia law. File this Claim Form, with Part A completed, with the Commission as soon as possible.

2. For questions or assistance with completing this form, please contact Customer Assistance using the Commission's toll-free number 877-664-2566.

3. If you are requesting a hearing, you must file medical reports supporting your request with the Commission. If you are requesting a hearing, complete Part B of this form and submit the medical reports either attached to the form, or as soon as possible.

4. If you are not requesting a hearing at this time, you may do so at a later date, but you should still submit this form with Part A completed. To request a hearing at a later date, please contact the Commission at 1-877-664-2566 or the Commission's website at *www.vwc.state.va.us* to obtain another copy of this form.

5. You may obtain copies of your medical records directly from your physician. Please contact **the Commission at 1-877-664-2566 for assistance.**

Employment Search Information Form

Date of Contact	Name/Address of Prospective Employer	Name of Contact Person	Type of Employment Sought	Outcome (i.e. Interview scheduled, no response, etc.)

Guidelines on Looking for Light-Duty Work

1. Good faith search for work – An employee who is partially disabled—i.e., unable to perform his or her regular job, but able to perform light duty work—is required to seek light duty work in good faith in order to receive disability benefits if he or she is not on an open award.

2. Factors the Commission considers – In deciding whether a partially disabled employee has made a reasonable effort to find suitable light duty employment the Commission considers such factors as: (1) the nature and extent of the disability; (2) the employee's training, age, experience and education; (3) the nature and extent of the job search; (4) the availability of jobs in the area suitable for the employee considering his disability; (5) any other matter affecting the employee's capacity to find suitable employment.

3. Evidence of reasonable effort – It is presumed that in most cases the claimant made a reasonable effort to market residual work capacity when he or she (a) registered with the Virginia Employment Commission within a reasonable time after being released to return to work and (b) directly contacted at least five potential employers per week where the employee has a reasonable basis to believe that there might be a job available that he or she might be able to perform[1] and (c) if appropriate, contacted the pre-injury employer for light duty work.

---

[1] It is not necessary to pre-screen or know for certain of the availability of a suitable job.

4. Keep a job search record – Information provided by the injured worker about job contacts should be supported by facts, preferably in writing, about the names of the employers contacted; where the employers are located; the date(s) the contact was made; whether the contact was in person, by phone or via internet; and the result of the contact.

5. Pre-injury skills or experience – Where an injured worker has particular job skills or training, he or she may focus the search on jobs in that field if there are jobs in that field that the employee can reasonably perform. However, if within a reasonable amount of time the search is not successful, the employee must broaden the search beyond that field.

6. Method of contacting employers – Employer contacts should be conducted in a manner reasonably suited to the position sought, which in some cases may be personal visits. In other cases, contacts may be by phone, internet, mail, or through employment agents such as union hiring halls.

7. Attempt to maximize earnings – If the employee locates and takes a job that pays substantially less than his or her pre-injury job, the employee should continue looking for a higher paying job.

Guidelines for Vocational Rehabilitation from The Virginia Workers' Compensation Commission

The Virginia Workers' Compensation Commission has issued these guidelines for vocational rehabilitation with the hope that the guidelines will provide better understanding between the parties, facilitate appropriate vocational rehabilitation, and eliminate needless conflict and litigation.

Neither the Virginia Workers' Compensation Act nor the regulations of the Commission have any provisions regarding the licensure or certification of rehabilitation counselors. Therefore, the Commission does no regulation on this point. Reference should be made to the provisions of Title 54.1 referenced in Section 65.2-603(A)(3) of the Workers' Compensation Act.

The Vocational Rehabilitation Plan

A. Vocational rehabilitation services, including vocational evaluation, counseling, job coaching, job development, job placement, on-the-job training, education, and retraining, shall take into account the employee's pre-injury job and wage classification; age, aptitude and level of education; the likelihood of success in the new vocation; and the relative costs and benefits of such services. Retraining should be considered if job placement efforts are not successful, or the employee's transferable skills are not readily marketable.

B. The provider should not ask the employee to engage in a job search or vocational rehabilitation until he/she is medically released for work. However, the provider may require the employee to meet in order to assess the employee's potential for work, and to prepare resumes and to schedule other appropriate actions, such as attending job preparation training, in anticipation of employment.

C. The two goals of vocational rehabilitation are to restore the employee to gainful employment, and to relieve the employer's burden of future compensation. Rehabilitation providers should attempt to find employment consistent with the employee's pre-injury position and salary level, and the provider should take into account such factors as distance, transportation costs, and actual anticipated earnings from the potential job, when considering such alternative employment.

D. It is the rehabilitation provider's responsibility to assess employment opportunities by direct contact with potential employers, and to determine whether a suitable position is presently available that is within the employee's restrictions and for which the employee is qualified. Until such prescreening contacts have been made to purge inappropriate leads, the provider should not ask the employee to attend interviews, but the provider may ask the employee to complete resumes and to attend job preparation training. The provider may ask the employee to attend interviews for present employment opportunities where it is anticipated that the employee will be released to such work within a reasonably brief period.

E. Telemarketing and commission sales positions are not appropriate job placement, unless the employee has demonstrated aptitude or ability in this line of work. Interviews with sheltered workshops and selective employers who are subsidized by employers/carriers are also inappropriate, if they do not provide the potential for legitimate rehabilitation, such as learning work skills or restoring the employee to a productive place in the labor market.

F. Requiring employees to look in newspapers, contact a specific number of potential employers per week, check listings at the VEC, or register with temporary services does not constitute appropriate "vocational rehabilitation." However, an employee may volunteer to do these activities. It would also be inappropriate for the rehabilitation provider to impose a blanket requirement on the employee to submit all job applications within twenty-four hours. It is not unreasonable for the provider to request written confirmation of the employee's job interviews or applications, when possible.

G. Rehabilitation providers may not advise the employee to withhold information about his/her injury or job capabilities during job interviews or on applications. However, the employee may not discuss them in such a way as to sabotage the interview or application process.

H. Employees are not required to give rehabilitation providers personal or financial information, such as number of children, spouse's employment, or credit history, unless such information relates to a *bona fide* occupational qualification for employment. An employee is required to disclose whether he/she is legally eligible for employment, has a valid driver's license, or has been convicted of a felony, and to provide his/her previous employment history.

Meetings Between Employees and Providers

A. Meetings should be held at reasonable times and places for both the employee and provider. Employees are not required to invite rehabilitation providers onto their property or into their homes. Also, just as the employee must cooperate with reasonable demands of the rehabilitation provider that are likely to return him/her to gainful employment, the provider must make reasonable accommodation for the employee's personal life.

B. Routine telephone contact should be made between 9:00 a.m. and 6:00 p.m. No calls should be made before 7:00 a.m. or after 10:00 p.m. except in cases of emergency.

C. The provider should give the employee advance notice, in writing, of meetings between the rehabilitation provider and employee, and of employment interviews. A minimum of five calendar days' notice of any meeting or employment interview is suggested, except for exceptional situations.

D. Prior to being released to light duty, the employee does not have to seek employment. However, the employee must meet with the provider to provide background information, to participate in an assessment of functional capacities in anticipation of a work release, and to satisfy other appropriate preparations for the vocational rehabilitation.

Role of Employee's Attorney

A. Employees have the right to have their attorney present at the initial rehabilitation meeting. However, an attorney may not delay such a meeting for more than two weeks nor can the attorney restrict contact between the employee and rehabilitation provider.

B. An employee may consult with his/her attorney at any time. Actions of the attorney will be imputed to the employee for the purposes of considering whether the employee is cooperating.

Medical Aspects of Rehabilitation

A. Neither the rehabilitation provider nor the carrier can medically manage the employee's treatment, by prescribing referrals, limiting treatment options, or otherwise participating in determining treatment unless requested by the physician.

B. Monitoring treatment is not medical management. With the consent of the physician, the provider may meet with the doctor outside of the employee's presence. The employee is not required to sign a consent granting the provider access to the physicians. If the physician does not wish to communicate with the provider, information may be obtained by utilizing discovery rights.

C. The employee has the right to a private examination by and consultation with the medical provider without the presence of the rehabilitation provider.

D. In order to determine the work capacity of the employee, the provider may require the employee to submit to a functional evaluation, if approved and authorized by the employee's treating physician or an independent medical examiner.

Transportation and Other Costs

A. The employee is entitled to reimbursement for expenses incurred in rehabilitation efforts. This includes mileage costs for trips to the VEC, rehabilitation meetings, obtaining or returning applications, attending interviews, and other travel at the direction of the provider. Costs incurred for telephone calls, photocopying, postage, and obtaining DMV and other records are also reimbursable, if such are requested by the rehabilitation provider or a potential employer.

B. When transportation is a problem, it is the responsibility of the vocational rehabilitation provider/carrier to make reasonable arrangements to insure the employee's attendance at meetings and interviews. This may include forwarding mileage money in advance or arranging appropriate alternative transportation, if requested.

INJURED WORKERS LAW FIRM

.

804-755-7755

7826 SHRADER ROAD

RICHMOND, VIRGINIA 23294

WWW.INJUREDWORKERSLAWFIRM.COM

INJURED WORKERS